THE WORLD'S GREAT SERMONS

HOOKER TO SOUTH

Volume II

Compiled by

GRENVILLE KLEISER

With an Introduction by

LEWIS O. BRASTOW

First published in 1908

British Library Cataloguing-in-Publication Data
A catalogue record for this book is available
from the British Library

CONTENTS

HOOKER

The Activity Of Faith; Or, Abraham's Imitators

JEREMY TAYLOR

Christ's Advent To Judgment

BAXTER

Making Light Of Christ And Salvation

BOSSUET

The Funeral Sermon
On The Death Of The Grande Condé

3

"The Lord Jesus Christ is the great Friend to whom we must all look for help, both for time and eternity."

—JOHN CHARLES RYLE

PREFACE

The aim in preparing this work has been to bring together the best examples of the products of the pulpit through the Christian centuries, and to present these masterpieces in attractive and convenient form. It is believed that they will be found valuable as instruction to ministers of to-day. They should also be helpful to others who, tho not preachers, yet seek reading of this kind for the upbuilding of personal character and for strengthening their Christian faith.

The sermons have been chosen in some cases for their literary and rhetorical excellences, but in every case for their helpfulness in solving some of the problems of Christian living. No two persons are likely to agree upon "the best" of anything, and readers will probably wish in particular instances that some other clergymen or sermons had been included. It is confidently believed, however, that the list here given is fairly representative of the preaching that characterized the age to which each sermon respectively belongs.

While some of the sermons of the early centuries may not seem exactly fitted to modern needs, it is thought that those presented will repay careful perusal, since they each contain a distinct message for later generations. Moreover, a comparison extending over the whole field of sermonic literature, such as the preacher may make with this collection before him, should prove most valuable as showing what progress and changes have come over homiletic matter and methods. Such a comparison should in fact throw much light on the spirit and conditions of various homiletic periods.

In choosing sermons by living preachers considerable difficulty has been found, not only in deciding upon sermons, but upon preachers. The list might have been extended indefinitely. Whenever possible the preacher, when living, has himself been consulted as to what he considered his most representative sermon.

Thanks are due, and are hereby acknowledged, to numerous clergymen, publishers, librarians, and others who have generously assisted the compiler in this undertaking. Most grateful acknowledgment is also made to the Rev. Epiphanius Wilson and the Rev. W.C. Stiles for valuable editorial assistance.

GRENVILLE KLEISER.
New York City, October, 1908.

INTRODUCTION

Collections of sermons by noted preachers of different periods are not an altogether uncommon contribution to literature. Italy, Germany, Holland, France, Great Britain and the United States have in this way furnished copious illustrations of the gifts of their illustrious preachers. Such treasures are found in the Latin and even in the Greek Church. Protestant communions especially, in line with the supreme significance which they attach to the work of the pulpit, have thus sought to magnify the calling and to perpetuate the memory and the influence of their distinguished sons. Still more comprehensive attempts have been made to collate the products of representative preachers in different Protestant communions, and thus to bring into prominence various types of sermonic literature. It is in this way that the Christian world has come to know its pulpit princes and to value their achievements.

The collection contained in the volumes before us is, however, more varied and comprehensive, reaching as it does from the fourth to the twentieth century, than any collection known to the writer. In the selection Professor Kleiser has brought to his task a personal knowledge of homiletic literature that is the product of much observation and study during many years, and an enthusiasm for his work that has been fostered by close intercourse in professional service with preachers and theological students. He has had the assistance also of men whose acquaintance with homiletic literature is very extensive, whose critical judgments are sound and reliable and who may be regarded as experts in this branch of knowledge. These volumes, therefore, may be accepted as a judiciously selected collection of sermons by many of the most notable preachers of the ancient and modern Christian world. Their value as illustrating varieties of gift, diversities of method, racial, national and ecclesiastical peculiarities, and above all progress in the science and art of preaching, may well be recognized even by a generation that is likely to regard anything that is more than twenty-four hours old as obsolete.

LEWIS O. BRASTOW.
Yale University, New Haven, Conn.,
October, 1908.

HOOKER

THE ACTIVITY OF FAITH; OR, ABRAHAM'S IMITATORS

BIOGRAPHICAL NOTE

Thomas Hooker, graduate and fellow of Cambridge, England, and practically founder of Connecticut, was born in 1586. He was dedicated to the ministry, and began his activities in 1620 by taking a small parish in Surrey. He did not, however, attract much notice for his powerful advocacy of reformed doctrine, until 1629, when he was cited to appear before Laud, the Bishop of London, whose threats induced him to leave England for Holland, whence he sailed with John Cotton, in 1633, for New England, and settled in Newtown, now Cambridge, Mass.

Chiefly in consequence of disagreements between his own and Cotton's congregation he, with a large following, migrated in 1636 to the Connecticut Valley, where the little band made their center at Hartford. Hooker was the inspirer if not the author of the Fundamental Laws and was of wide political as well as religious influence in organizing "The United Colonies of New England" in 1643—the first effort after federal government made on this continent. He was an active preacher and prolific writer up to his death in 1647.

HOOKER

1586-1647
THE ACTIVITY OF FAITH;
OR, ABRAHAM'S IMITATORS

And the father of circumcision to them who are not of circumcision only, but who also walk in the steps of that faith of our father Abraham, which he had, being yet uncircumcized.
—Romans iv., 12.

I proceed now to show who those are, that may, and do indeed, receive benefit as Abraham did. The text saith, "They that walk in the steps of that faith of Abraham:" that man that not only enjoyeth the privileges of the Church, but yieldeth the obedience of faith, according to the Word of God revealed, and walketh in obedience, *that* man alone shall be blest with faithful Abraham.

Two points may be here raised, but I shall hardly handle them both; therefore I will pass over the first only with a touch, and that lieth closely couched in the text.

That faith causeth fruitfulness in the hearts and lives of those in whom it is.

Mark what I say: a faithful man is a fruitful man; faith enableth a man to be doing. Ask the question, by what power was it whereby Abraham was enabled to yield obedience to the Lord? The text answereth you, "They that walk in the footsteps" not of Abraham, but "in the footsteps of the faith of Abraham." A man would have thought the text should have run thus: They that walk in the footsteps of Abraham. That is true, too, but the apostle had another end; therefore he saith, "They that walk in the footsteps of the faith of Abraham," implying that it was the

13

grace of faith that God bestowed on Abraham, that quickened and enabled him to perform every duty that God required of him, and called him to the performance of. So that I say, the question being, whence came it that Abraham was so fruitful a Christian, what enabled him to do and to suffer what he did? surely it was faith that was the cause that produced such effects, that helped him to perform such actions. The point then you see is evident, faith it is that causeth fruit.

Hence it is, that of almost all the actions that a Christian hath to do, faith is still said to be the worker. If a man pray as he should, it is "the prayer of faith." If a man obey as he should, it is the obedience of faith. If a man war in the Church militant, it is "the fight of faith." If a man live as a Christian and holy man, he "liveth by faith." Nay, shall I say yet more, if he died as he ought, "he dieth by faith." "These all died in faith." What is that? The power of faith that directed and ordered them in the cause of their death, furnished them with grounds and principles of assurance of the love of God, made them carry themselves patiently in death. I can say no more, but with the apostle, "Examine yourselves, whether ye be in the faith." Why doth not the apostle say, Examine whether faith be in you, but "whether ye be in the faith"? His meaning is, that as a man is said to be in drink, or to be in love, or to be in passion, that is, under the command of drink, or love, or passion; so the whole man must be under the command of faith (as you shall see more afterward). If he prays, faith must indite his prayer; if he obey, faith must work; if he live, it is faith that must quicken him; and if he die, it is faith that must order him in death. And wheresoever faith is, it will do wonders in the soul of that man where it is; it can not be idle; it will have footsteps, it sets the whole man on work; it moveth feet, and hands, and eyes, and all parts of the body. Mark how the apostle disputeth: "We having the same spirit of faith, according as it is written, I believed, and therefore have I spoken, we also believe, and therefore speak." The faith of the apostle, which he had in his heart, set his tongue agoing. If a man have faith within, it will break forth at his mouth. This shall suffice for the proof of the point; I thought to have prest it further, but if I should, I see the time would prevent me.

The use, therefore, in a word, is this: if this be so, then it falleth foul, and is a heavy bill of indictment against many that live in the bosom of the Church. Go thy ways home, and read but this text, and consider seriously but this one thing in it: That whosoever is the son of Abraham, hath faith, and whosoever hath faith is a walker, is a marker; by the footsteps of faith you may see where faith hath been. Will not this, then, I say, fall marvelous heavy upon many souls that live in the bosom of the Church, who are confident, and put it out of all question, that they are true believers, and make no doubt but what they have faith? But look to it, wheresoever faith is, it is fruitful. If thou art fruitless, say what thou wilt, thou hast no faith at all. Alas, these idle drones, these idle Christians, the Church is too full of them; Men are continually hearing, and yet remain fruitless and unprofitable; whereas if there were more faith in the world, we should have more work done in the world; faith would set feet, and hands, and eyes, and all on work. Men go under the name of professors, but alas! they are but pictures; they stir not a whit; mark, where you found them in the beginning of the year, there you shall find them in the end of the year, as profane, as worldly, as loose in their conversations, as formal in duty as ever. And is this faith? Oh! faith would work other matters, and provoke a soul to other passages than these.

But you will say, may not a man have faith, and not that fruit you speak of? May not a man have a good heart to Godward, altho he can not find that ability in matter of fruitfulness?

My brethren, be not deceived; such an opinion is a mere delusion of Satan; wherever faith is it bringeth Christ into the soul; mark that, "Whosoever believeth, Christ dwelleth in his heart by faith. And if Christ be in you," saith the apostle, "the body is dead, because of sin, but the spirit is life, because of righteousness." If Christ be in you, that is, whosoever believeth in the Lord Jesus, Christ dwells in such a man by faith; now if Christ be in the soul, the body can not be dead; but a man is alive, and quick, and active to holy duties, ready, and willing, and cheerful in the performance of whatsoever God requireth. Christ is not a dear Savior, nor the Spirit a dead Spirit: the second Adam is made a quickening spirit. And wherever the Spirit is, it works effects suitable to itself. The Spirit is a spirit of purity, a spirit of zeal, and where it is it maketh pure and zealous. When a man will say he hath faith, and in the mean time can be content to be idle and unfruitful in the work of the Lord, can be content to be a dead Christian, let him know that his case is marvelously fearful: for if faith were in him indeed it would appear; ye can not keep your good hearts to yourselves; wherever fire is it will burn, and wherever faith is it can not be kept secret. The heart will be enlarged, the soul quickened, and there will be a change in the whole life and conversation, if ever faith takes place in a man. I will say no more of this, but proceed to the second point arising out of the affirmative part.

You will say, what fruit is it then? Or how shall a man know what is the true fruit of faith, indeed, whereby he may discern his own estate? I answer, the text will tell you: "He that walketh in the footsteps of that faith of Abraham." By footsteps are meant the works the actions, the holy endeavors of Abraham; and where those footsteps are there is the faith of Abraham. So that the point of instruction hence is thus much (which indeed is the main drift of the apostle).

That, Every faithful man may, yea doth, imitate the actions of faithful Abraham.

Mark what I say; I say again, this is to be the son of Abraham, not because we are begotten of him by natural generation, for so the Jews are the sons of Abraham; but Abraham is our father because he is the pattern, for the proceeding of our faith. "Thy father was an Amorite," saith the Scripture: that is, thou followest the steps of the Amorites in thy conversation. So is Abraham called the "father of the faithful," because he is the copy of their course, whom they must follow in those services that God calleth for. So the point is clear, every faithful man may, yea doth, and must imitate the actions of faithful Abraham. It is Christ's own plea, and He presseth it as an undeniable truth upon the hearts of the Scribes and Pharisees, that bragged very highly of their privileges and prerogatives, and said, "Abraham is our father." "No (saith Christ), if ye were Abraham's children ye would do the works of Abraham." To be like Abraham in constitution, to be one of his blood, is not that which makes a man a son of Abraham, but to be like him in holiness of affection, to have a heart framed and a life disposed answerably to his. The apostle in like manner presseth this point when he would provoke the Hebrews, to whom he wrote, to follow the examples of the saints: "Whose faith (says he) follow, considering the end of their conversation." So the apostle Peter presseth the example of Sarah upon all good women: "Whose daughter ye are (saith he) as long: as ye do well."

For the opening of the point, and that ye may more clearly understand it, a question here would be resolved, what were "the footsteps of the faith of Abraham"? which way went he? This is a question, I say, worthy the scanning, and therefore (leaving the further confirmation of the point, as already evident enough) I will come to it that you may know what to settle your hearts upon.

I answer, therefore, there are six footsteps of the faith of Abraham, which are the main things wherein every faithful man must do as Abraham did, in the work of faith—I mean in his ordinary course; for if there be any thing extraordinary no man is bound to imitate him therein; but in the works of faith, I say, which belongeth to all men, every man must imitate Abraham in these six steps, and then he is in the next door to happiness, the very next neighbor, as I say, to heaven.

The first advance which Abraham made in the ways of grace and happiness, you shall observe to be a yielding to the call of God. Mark what God said to Abraham: "Get thee out of thy country, and from thy kindred, and from thy father's house, unto a land that I will show thee; and Abraham departed," saith the text, "as the Lord had spoken unto him." Even when he was an idolater, he is content to lay aside all and let the command of God bear the sway; neither friends, nor kindred, nor gods can keep him back, but he presently stoopeth to the call of God. So it is, my brethren, with every faithful man. This is his first step: he is content to be under the rule and power of God's command. Let the Lord call for him, require any service of him, his soul presently yieldeth, and is content to be framed and fashioned to God's call, and returneth an obedient answer thereto; he is content to come out of his sins, and out of himself, and to receive the impressions of the Spirit. This is that which God requireth, not only of Abraham, but of all believers: "Whosoever will be my disciple," saith Christ, "must forsake father, and mother, and children, and houses, and lands"; yea, and he must "deny himself, and take up his cross and follow me." This is the first step in Christianity, to lay down our own honors, to trample upon our own respects, to submit our necks to the block, as it were, and whatever God commands, to be content that His good pleasure should take place with us.

Then Abraham, as doth every faithful soul, set forward, in this wise: He showed that whenever faith cometh powerfully into the heart, the soul is not content barely to yield to the command of God, but it breatheth after His mercy, longeth for His grace, prizeth Christ and salvation above all things in the world, is satisfied and contented with nothing but with the Lord Christ, and altho it partake of many things below, and enjoy abundance of outward comforts, yet it is not quieted till it rest and pitch itself upon the Lord, and find and feel that evidence and assurance of His love, which He hath promised unto and will bestow on those who love Him. As for all things here below, he hath but a slight, and mean, and base esteem of them. This you shall see apparent in Abraham. "Fear not, Abraham (saith God), I am thy shield, and thy exceeding great reward." What could a man desire more? One would think that the Lord makes a, promise here large enough to Abraham, "I will be thy buckler, and exceeding great reward." Is not Abraham contented with this? No; mark how he pleadeth with God: "Lord God (saith he), what wilt thou give me, seeing I go childless?" His eye is upon the promise that God had made to him of a son, of whom the Savior of the world should come. "O Lord, what wilt thou give me?" as if he had said, What wilt Thou do for me? alas! nothing will do my soul good unless I have a son, and in him a Savior. What will become of me so long as I go childless, and so Saviorless, as I may so speak? You see how Abraham's mouth was out of taste with all other things, how he could relish nothing, enjoy nothing in comparison of the promise, tho he had otherwise what he would, or could desire. Thus must it be with every faithful man. That soul never had, nor never shall have Christ, that doth not prize Him above all things in the world.

The next step of Abraham's faith was this, he casteth himself and flingeth his soul, as I may say, upon the all-sufficient power and mercy of God for the attainment of what he desireth; he rolleth and tumbleth himself, as it were, upon the all-sufficiency of God. This you shall find in Rom. iv. 18, where the apostle, speaks of Abraham, who "against hope, believed in hope"; that is, when there was no hope in the world, yet he believed in God, even above hope, and so made it possible. It was an object of his hope, that it might be in regard of God, howsoever there was no possibility in regard of man. So the text saith, "he considered not his own body now dead, when he was about a hundred years old, neither yet the deadness of Sarah's womb, but was strong in faith." He cast himself wholly upon the precious promise and mercy of God.

But he took another step in true justifying faith. He proved to us the believer is informed touching the excellency of the Lord Jesus, and that fulness that is to be had in Him, tho he can not find the sweetness of His mercy, tho he can not or dare not apprehend and apply it to himself, tho he find nothing in himself, yet he is still resolved to rest upon the Lord, and to stay himself on the God of his salvation, and to wait for His mercy till he find Him gracious to his poor soul. Excellent and famous is the example of the woman of Canaan. When Christ, as it were, beat her off, and took up arms against her, was not pleased to reveal Himself graciously to her for the present, "I am not sent (saith He) but to the lost sheep of the house of Israel; and it is not meet to take the children's bread, and to cast it to the dogs"; mark how she replied, "Truth, Lord, I confess all that; yet notwithstanding, the dogs eat of the crumbs that fall from their master's table." Oh, the excellency, and strength, and work of her faith! She comes to Christ for mercy, He repelleth her, reproacheth her, tells her she is a dog; she confesseth her baseness, is not discouraged for all that, but still resteth upon the goodness and mercy of Christ, and is mightily resolved to have mercy whatsoever befalleth her. Truth, Lord, I confess I am as bad as Thou canst term me, yet I confess, too, that there is no comfort but from Thee, and tho I am a dog, yet I would have crumbs. Still she laboreth to catch after mercy, and to lean and to bear herself upon the favor of Christ for the bestowing thereof upon her. So it must be with every faithful Christian in this particular; he must roll himself upon the power, and faithfulness, and truth of God, and wait for His mercy (I will join them both together for brevity's sake, tho the latter be a fourth step and degree of faith); I say he must not only depend upon God, but he must wait upon the Holy One of Israel.

But a further step of Abraham's faith appeared in this: he counted nothing too dear for the Lord; he was content to break through all impediments, to pass through all difficulties, whatsoever God would have, He had of him. This is the next step that Abraham went; and this you shall find when God put him upon trial. The text saith there "that God did tempt Abraham," did try what He would do for Him, and He bade him, "Go, take thy son, thine only son, Isaac, whom thou lovest, and slay him"; and straight Abraham went and laid his son upon an altar, and took a knife, to cut the throat of his son—so that Abraham did not spare his son Isaac, he did not spare for any cost, he did not dodge with God in this case; if God would have anything, He should have it, whatsoever it were, tho it were his own life, for no question Isaac was dearer to him than his own life. And this was not his case alone, but the faithful people of God have ever walked the same course. The apostle Paul was of the same spirit; "I know not (saith he) the things that shall befall me, save that the Holy Ghost witnesseth in every city, saying that bonds and afflictions abide me: but none of these things move me, neither count I my life dear unto myself, so that I might finish my course with joy, and the ministry which I have received of the Lord Jesus, to testify the Gospel of the grace of God." O blest spirit! here is the work of faith. Alas! when we come to part with anything for the cause of God, how hardly comes it from us! "But I (saith he) pass not, no, nor is my life dear unto me." Here, I say, is the work of faith, indeed, when a man is content to do anything for God, and to say if imprisonment, loss of estate, liberty, life, come, I pass not, it moveth me nothing, so I may finish my course with comfort. Hence it was that the saints of God in those primitive times "took joyfully the spoiling of their goods." Methinks I see the saints there reaching after Christ with the arms of faith, and how, when anything lay in their way, they were content to lose all, to part with all, to have Christ. Therefore saith Saint Paul, "I am ready not to be bound only, but also to die at Jerusalem for the name of the Lord Jesus." Mark, rather than he would leave his Savior, he would leave his life, and tho men would have hindered him, yet was resolved to have Christ, howsoever, tho he lost his life for Him. Oh, let me have my Savior, and take my life!

The last step of all is this: when the soul is thus resolved not to dodge with God, but to part with anything for Him, then in the last place there followeth a readiness of heart to address man's self to the performance of whatsoever duty God requireth at his hands; I say this is the last step, when, without consulting with flesh and blood, without hammering upon it, as it were, without awkwardness of heart, there followeth a readiness to obey God; the soul is at hand. When Abraham was called, "Behold (saith he) here I am." And so Samuel, "Speak, Lord, for thy servant heareth," and so Ananias. "Behold, I am here, Lord." The faithful soul is not to seek, as an evil servant that is gone a roving after his companions, that is out of the way when his master would use him, but is like a trusty servant that waiteth upon his master, and is ever at hand to do His pleasure. So you shall see it was with Abraham, when the Lord commanded him to go out of his country, "he obeyed, and went out, not knowing whither he went"; he went cheerfully and readily, tho he knew not whither; as who would say, if the Lord calls, I will not question, if He command I will perform, whatever it be. So it must be with every faithful soul—we must blind the eye of carnal reason, resolve to obey, tho heaven and earth seem to meet together in a contradiction, care not what man or what devil saith in this case, but what God will have done, do it; this is the courage and obedience of faith. See how Saint Paul, in the place before named, flung his ancient friends from him, when they came to cross him in the work of his ministry. They all came about him, and because they thought they should see his face no more, they besought him not to go up to Jerusalem. Then Paul answered, "What, mean ye to weep, and to break my heart?" as who should say, It is a grief and a vexation to my soul, that ye would burden me, that I can not go with readiness to perform the service that God requireth at my hands. The like Christian courage was in Luther when his friends dissuaded him to go to Worms: "If all the tiles in 'Worms' were so many devils (said he) yet would I go thither in the name of my Lord Jesus." This is the last step.

Now gather up a little what I have delivered. He that is resolved to stoop to the call of God; to prize the promises, and breathe after them; to rest upon the Lord, and to wait His time for bestowing mercy upon him; to break through all impediments and difficulties, and to count nothing too dear for God; to be content to perform ready and cheerful obedience; he that walketh thus, and treadeth in these steps, peace be upon him; heaven is hard by; he is as sure of salvation as the angels are; it is as certain as the Lord liveth that he shall be saved with faithful Abraham, for he walketh in the steps of Abraham, and therefore he is sure to be where he is. The case, you see, is clear, and the point evident, that every faithful man may, and must, imitate faithful Abraham.

It may be here imagined, that we draw men up to too high a pitch; and certainly, if this be the sense of the words, and the meaning of the Holy Ghost in this place, what will become of many that live in the bosom of the Church? Will you therefore see the point confirmed by reason? The ground of this doctrine stands thus: every faithful man hath the same faith, for nature and for work, that Abraham had; therefore, look what nature his faith was of, and what power it had; of the same nature and power every true believer's faith is. Briefly thus: the promises of God are the ground upon which all true faith resteth; the Spirit of God it is that worketh this faith in all believers; the power of the Spirit is that that putteth forth itself in the hearts and lives of all the faithful; gather these together: if all true believers have the same promises for the ground of their faith; have one and the same spirit to work it; have' one and the same power to draw out the abilities of faith, then certainly they can not but have the very self-same actions, having the very self-same ground of their actions.

Every particular believer (as the apostle Peter saith) "hath obtained the like precious faith." Mark, that there is a great deal of copper faith in the world—much counterfeit believing; but the saints do all partake of "the like precious faith." As when a man hath but a sixpence in silver, or a crown in gold, those small pieces, for the nature, are as good as the greatest of the same metal; so it is with the faith of God's elect. And look as it is in grafting; if there be many scions of the same kind grafted into one stock, they all partake alike of the virtue of the stock; just so it is here. The Lord Jesus Christ is the stock, as it were, into which all the faithful are grafted by the spirit of God and faith; therefore, whatsoever fruit one beareth, another beareth also:

23

howsoever, there may be degrees of works, yet they are of the same nature. As a little apple is the same in taste with a great one of the same tree, even so every faithful man hath the same holiness of heart and life, because he hath the same principle of holiness. The fruit indeed that one Christian bringeth may be but poor and small in comparison with others, yet it is the same in kind; the course of his life is not with so much power and fulness of grace, it may be, as another's, yet there is the same true grace, and the same practise, in the kind of it, for truth, however in degree it differ.

Let us now come to see what benefit we may make to ourselves of this point, thus proved and confirmed; and, certainly, the use of this doctrine is of great consequence. In the first place, it is a just ground of examination. For if it be true (as can not be denied, the reasons being so strong, and arguments so plain) that every son of Abraham followeth the steps of Abraham, then here you may clearly perceive who it is that hath saving faith indeed, who they be that are true saints and the sons of Abraham. By the light of this truth, by the rule of this doctrine, if you would square your courses, and look into your conversations, you can not but discern whether you have faith or no. That man whose faith showeth itself and putteth itself forth in its several conditions, agreeably to, the faith of Abraham, that man that followeth the footsteps of the faith of Abraham, let him be esteemed a faithful man, let him be reckoned for a true believer.

You that are gentlemen and tradesmen, I appeal to your souls whether the Lord and His cause is not the loser this way? Doth not prayer pay for it? Doth not the Word pay for it? Are not the ordinances always losers when anything of your own cometh in competition? Is it not evident, then, that you are not under the command of the Word? How do you tremble at the wrath and threatenings of a mortal man? and yet, when you hear the Lord thunder judgments out of His Word, who is humbled? When He calls for fasting, and weeping, and mourning, who regards it? Abraham, my brethren, did not thus: these were none of his steps; no, no: he went a hundred miles off this course. The Lord no sooner said to him, "Forsake thy country and thy kindred, and thy father's house," but he forsook all, neither friend nor father prevailed to detain him from obedience, but he stooped willingly to God's command.

There are a sort that come short of being the sons of Abraham, and they are the close-hearted hypocrites. These are a generation that are of a more refined kind than the last, but howsoever they carry the matter very covertly, yea, and are exceeding cunning; yet the truth will make them known. Many a hypocrite may come thus far, to be content to part with anything, and outwardly to suffer for the cause of God, to part with divers pleasures and lusts, and to perform many holy services. But here is the difference between Abraham and these men: Abraham forsook his goods and all, but your close-hearted hypocrites have always some god or other that they do homage to—their ease, or their wealth, or some secret lust, something or other they have set up as an idol within them—and so long as they may have and enjoy that, they will part with anything else. But thou must know that, if thou be one of Abraham's children, thou must come away from thy gods—the god of pride, of self-love, of vainglory—and leave worshiping of these, and be content to be alone by God and His truth. This shall suffice for the first use; I can not proceed further in the pressing thereof, because I would shut up all with the time.

The second use is a word of instruction, and it shall be but a word or two; that if all the saints of God must walk in the same way of life and salvation that Abraham did, then there is no byway to bring a man to happiness. Look, what way Abraham went, you must go; there are no more ways: the same course that he took must be a copy for you to follow, a rule, as it were, for you to square your whole conversation by. There is no way but one to come to life and happiness. I speak it the rather to dash that idle device of many carnal men, that think the Lord hath a new invention to bring them to life, and that they need not go the ordinary way, but God hath made a shorter cut for them. Great men and gentlemen think God will spare them. What, must they be humbled, and fast, and pray! That is for poor men, and mean men. Their places and estates will not suffer it; therefore surely God hath given a dispensation to them. And the poor men, they think it is for gentlemen that have more leisure and time: alas! they live by their labor, and they must take pains for what they have, and therefore they can not do what is required. But be not deceived; if there be any way beside that which Abraham went, then will I deny myself. But the case is clear, the Lord saith it, the Word saith it; the same way, the same footsteps that Abraham took, we must take, if ever we will come where Abraham is.

You must not balk in this kind, whoever you are; God respecteth no man's person. If you would arrive at the same haven, you must sail through the same sea. You must walk the same way of grace, if you would come to the same kingdom of glory. It is a conceit that harboreth in the hearts of many men, nay, of most men in general, especially your great wise men and your great rich men, that have better places and estates in the world than ordinary. What, think they, may not a man be saved without all this ado? What needs all this? Is there not another way besides this? Surely, my brethren, you must teach our Savior Christ and the apostle Paul another way. I am sure they never knew another; and he that dreameth of another way must be content to go beside. There is no such matter as the devil would persuade you; it is but his delusion to keep you under infidelity, and so shut you up to destruction under false and vain conceits. The truth is, here is the way, and the only way, and you must walk here if ever you come to life and happiness. Therefore, be not deceived, suffer not your eyes to be blinded; but know, what Abraham did, you must do the same, if not in action, yet in affection. If God say, forsake all, thou must do it, at least in affection. Thou must still wait upon His power and providence; yield obedience to Him in all things; be content to submit thyself to His will. This is the way you must walk in, if you ever come to heaven.

The last use shall be a use of comfort to all the saints and people of God, whose consciences can witness that they have labored to walk in the uprightness of their heart as Abraham did. I have two or three words to speak to these.

Be persuaded out of the Word of God, that your course is good, and go on with comfort, and the God of heaven be with you; and be sure of it, that you that walk with Abraham shall be at rest with Abraham; and it shall never repent you of all the pains that you have taken. Haply it may seem painful and tedious to you; yet, what Abigail said to David, let me say to you: "Oh," saith she, "let not my lord do this: when the Lord shall have done to my lord according to all the good that he hath spoken concerning thee, and shall have appointed thee ruler over Israel, this shall be no grief unto thee, nor offense of heart, that thou hast shed blood causeless, or that my lord hath avenged himself." My brethren, let me say to you, you will find trouble and inconveniences and hard measure at the hands of the wicked in this world. Many Nabals and Cains will set themselves against you; but go on, and bear it patiently. Know it is a troublesome way, but a true way; it is grievous but yet good; and the end will be happy. It will never repent you, when the Lord hath performed all the good that He hath spoken concerning you.

Oh! to see a man drawing his breath low and short, after he hath spent many hours and days in prayer to the Lord, grappling with his corruptions, and striving to pull down his base lusts, after he hath waited upon the Lord in a constant course of obedience. Take but such a man, and ask him, now his conscience is opened, whether the ways of holiness and sincerity be not irksome to him, whether he be not grieved with himself for undergoing so much needless trouble (as the world thinks it); and his soul will then clear this matter. It is true he hath a tedious course of it, but now his death will be blest. He hath striven for a crown, and now beholds a crown. Now he is beyond the waves. All the contempts, and imprisonments, and outrages of wicked men are now too short to reach him. He is so far from repenting, that he rejoiceth and triumpheth in reflecting back upon all the pains, and care, and labor of love, whereby he hath loved the Lord Jesus, in submitting his heart unto Him.

Take me another man, that hath lived here in pomp and jollity, hath had many livings, great preferments, much honor, abundance of pleasure, yet hath been ever careless of God and of His Word, profane in his course, loose in his conversation, and ask him upon his deathbed, how it standeth with him. Oh! woe the time, that ever he spent it as he hath done. Now the soul begins to hate the man, and the very sight of him that hath been, the instrument with it in the committing of sin. Now nothing but gall and wormwood remaineth. Now the sweetness of the adulterer's lust is gone, and nothing but the sting of conscience remaineth. Now the covetous man must part with his goods, and the gall of asps must stick behind. Now the soul sinks within, and the heart is overwhelmed with sorrow. Take but these two men, I say, and judge by their ends, whether it will ever repent you that you have done well, that you have walked in the steps of the faith of Abraham.

My brethren, howsoever you have had many miseries, yet the Lord hath many mercies for you. God dealeth with His servants, as a father doth with his son, after he hath sent him on a journey to do some business; and the weather falleth foul, and the way proveth dangerous, and many a storm, and great difficulties are to be gone through. Oh, how the heart of that father pitieth his son! How doth he resolve to requite him, if he ever live to come home again! What preparation doth he make to entertain, and welcome him; and how doth he study to do good unto him! My brethren, so it is here; I beseech you, think of it, you that are the saints and people of God. You must find in your way many troubles and griefs (and we ought to find them), but be not discouraged. The more misery, the greater mercy. God the Father seeth His servants: and if they suffer and endure for a good conscience, as His eye seeth them, so His soul pitieth them. His heart bleeds within Him for them; that is, He hath a tender compassion of them, and He saith within Himself, Well,

I will requite them if ever they come into My kingdom; all their patience, and care, and conscience in walking My ways, I will requite; and they shall receive a double reward from Me, even a crown of eternal glory. Think of these things that are not seen; they are eternal. The things that are seen are temporal, and they will deceive us. Let our hearts be carried after the other, and rest in them forever!

JEREMY TAYLOR

CHRIST'S ADVENT TO JUDGMENT

BIOGRAPHICAL NOTE

Jeremy Taylor, born in Cambridge, England, in 1613, was the son of a barber. By his talents he obtained an entrance into Caius College, where his exceptional progress obtained for him admission to the ministry in his twenty-first year, two years before the canonical age. He was appointed in succession fellow of All Souls, Oxford, through the influence of Laud, chaplain to the King, and rector of Uppingham. During the Commonwealth he was expelled from his living and opened a school in Wales, employing his seclusion in writing his memorable work "The Liberty of Prophesying."

At the Restoration, Charles II raised him to the bishopric of Down and Connor (1660), in which post he remained until his death in 1667. His *"Ductor Dubitantium,"* dedicated to Charles II, is a work of subtilty and ingenuity; his "Holy Living" and "Holy Dying" (1652), are unique monuments of learning and devotion. His sermons form, however, his most brilliant and most voluminous productions, and fully establish his claims to the first place among the learned, witty, fanciful, ornate and devotional prose writers of his time.

JEREMY TAYLOR

1613-1667
CHRIST'S ADVENT TO JUDGMENT

For we must all appear before the judgment seat of Christ, that every one may receive the things done in his body, according to that he hath done, whether it be good or bad.—II Cor., v., 10.

If we consider the person of the Judge, we first perceive that He is interested in the injury of the crimes He is to sentence: "They shall look on Him whom they have pierced." It was for thy sins that the Judge did suffer such unspeakable pains as were enough to reconcile all the world to God; the sum and spirit of which pains could not be better understood than by the consequence of His own words, "My God, my God, why hast thou forsaken me?" meaning, that He felt such horrible, pure, unmingled sorrows, that, altho His human nature was personally united to the Godhead, yet at that instant he felt no comfortable emanations by sensible perception from the Divinity, but He was so drenched in sorrow that the Godhead seemed to have forsaken Him. Beyond this, nothing can be added: but then, that thou hast for thy own particular made all this sin in vain and ineffective, that Christ thy Lord and Judge should be tormented for nothing, that thou wouldst not accept felicity and pardon when he purchased them at so dear a price, must needs be an infinite condemnation to such persons. How shalt thou look upon Him that fainted and died for love of thee, and thou didst scorn His miraculous mercies? How shall we dare to behold that holy face that brought salvation to us, and we turned away and fell in love with death, and kissed deformity and sins? And yet in the beholding that face consists much of the glories of eternity. All the pains and passions, the sorrows and the groans, the humility and poverty, the labors and watchings, the prayers and the sermons, the miracles and the prophecies, the whip and the nails, the death and the burial, the shame and the smart, the cross and the grave of Jesus, shall be laid upon thy score, if thou hast refused the mercies and design of all their holy ends and purposes. And if we remember what a calamity that was which broke the Jewish nation in pieces, when Christ came to judge them for their murdering Him who was their King and the Prince of Life, and consider that this was but a dark image of the terrors of the day of judgment, we may then apprehend that there is some strange unspeakable evil that attends them that are guilty of this death, and of so much evil to their Lord. Now it is certain if thou wilt not be saved by His death, you are guilty of His death; if thou wilt not suffer Him to have thee, thou art guilty of destroying Him; and then let it be considered what is to be expected from that Judge before whom you stand as His murderer and betrayer. But this is but half of this consideration.

Christ may be crucified again, and upon a new account, put to an open shame. For after that Christ has done all this by the direct actions of His priestly office, of sacrificing himself for us, He hath also done very many things for us which are also the fruits of His first love and prosecutions of our redemption. I will not instance the strange arts of mercy that our Lord uses to bring us to live holy lives; but I consider, that things are so ordered, and so great a value set upon our souls since they are the images of God, and redeemed by the blood of the Holy Lamb, that the salvation of our souls is reckoned as a part of Christ's reward, a part of the glorification of His humanity. Every sinner that repents causes joy to Christ, and the joy is so great that it runs over and wets the fair brows and beauteous looks of cherubim and seraphim, and all the angels have a part of that banquet; then it is that our blest Lord feels the fruits of His holy death; the acceptation of His holy sacrifice, the graciousness of His person, the return of His prayers. For all that Christ did or suffered, and all that He now does as a priest in heaven, is to glorify His Father by bringing souls to God. For this it was that He was born and died, that He descended from heaven to earth, from life to death, from the cross to the grave; this was the purpose of His resurrection and ascension, of the end and design of all the miracles and graces of God manifested to all the world by Him; and now what man is so vile, such a malicious fool, that will refuse to bring joy to his Lord by doing himself the greatest good in the world? They who refuse to do this, are said to crucify the Lord of Life again, and put him to an open shame—that is, they, as much as in them lies, bring Christ from His glorious joys to the labors of His life and the shame of His death; they advance His enemies, and refuse to advance the kingdom of their Lord; they put themselves in that state in which they were when Christ came to die for them; and now that He is in a state that He may rejoice over them (for He hath done all His share towards it), every wicked man takes his head from the blessing, and rather chooses that the devils should rejoice in his destruction, than that his Lord should triumph in his felicity. And now upon the supposition of these premises, we may imagine that it will be an infinite amazement to meet that Lord to be our Judge whose person we have murdered, whose honor we have disparaged, whose purposes we have destroyed, whose joys we have lessened, whose passion we have made ineffectual, and whose love we have trampled under our profane and impious feet.

But there is yet a third part of this consideration. As it will be inquired at the day of judgment concerning the dishonors to the person of Christ, so also concerning the profession and institution of Christ, and concerning His poor members; for by these also we make sad reflections upon our Lord. Every man that lives wickedly disgraces the religion and institution of Jesus, he discourages strangers from entering into it, he weakens the hands of them that are in already, and makes that the adversaries speak reproachfully of the name of Christ; but altho it is certain our Lord and Judge will deeply resent all these things, yet there is one thing which He takes more tenderly, and that is, the uncharitableness of men towards His poor. It shall then be upbraided to them by the Judge, that Himself was hungry and they refused to give meat to Him that gave them His body and heart-blood to feed them and quench their thirst; that they denied a robe to cover His nakedness, and yet He would have clothed their souls with the robe of His righteousness, lest their souls should be found naked on the day of the Lord's visitation; and all this unkindness is nothing but that evil men were uncharitable to their brethren, they would not feed the hungry, nor give drink to the thirsty nor clothe the naked, nor relieve their brothers' needs, nor forgive their follies, nor cover their shame, nor turn their eyes from delighting in their affronts and evil accidents; this is it which our Lord will take so tenderly, that His brethren for whom He died, who sucked the paps of His mother, that fed on His body and are nourished with His blood, whom He hath lodged in His heart and entertains in His bosom, the partners of His spirit and co-heirs of His inheritance, that these should be denied relief and suffered to go away ashamed, and unpitied; this our blest Lord will take so ill, that all those who are guilty of this unkindness, have no reason to expect the favor of the Court.

To this if we add the almightiness of the Judge, His infinite wisdom and knowledge of all causes, and all persons, and all circumstances, that He is infinitely just, inflexibly angry, and impartial in His sentence, there can be nothing added either to the greatness or the requisites of a terrible and an almighty Judge. For who can resist Him who is almighty? Who can evade His scrutiny that knows all things? Who can hope for pity of Him that is inflexible? Who can think to be exempted when the Judge is righteous and impartial? But in all these annexes of the Great Judge, that which I shall now remark, is that indeed which hath terror in it, and that is, the severity of our Lord. For then is the day of vengeance and recompenses, and no mercy at all shall be showed, but to them that are the sons of mercy; for the other, their portion is such as can be expected from these premises.

If we remember the instances of God's severity in this life, in the days of mercy and repentance, in those days when judgment waits upon mercy, and receives laws by the rules and measures of pardon, and that for all the rare streams of loving; kindness issuing out of paradise and refreshing all our fields with a moisture more fruitful than the floods of Nilus, still there are mingled some storms and violences, some fearful instances of the divine justice, we may more readily expect it will be worse, infinitely worse, at that day, when judgment shall ride in triumph, and mercy shall be the accuser of the wicked. But so we read, and are commanded to remember, because they are written for our example, that God destroyed at once five cities of the plain, and all the country, and Sodom and her sisters are set forth for an example, suffering the vengeance of eternal fire. Fearful it was when God destroyed at once twenty-three thousand for fornication, and an exterminating angel in one night killed one hundred and eighty-five thousand of the Assyrians, and the first-born of all the families of Egypt, and for the sin of David in numbering the people, three score and ten thousand of the people died, and God sent ten tribes into captivity and eternal oblivion and indistinction from a common people for their idolatry. Did not God strike Korah and his company with fire from heaven? and the earth opened and swallowed up the congregation of Abiram? And is not evil come upon all the world for one sin of Adam? Did not the anger of God break the nation of the Jews all in pieces with judgments so great, that no nation ever suffered the like, because none ever sinned so? And at once it was done, that God in anger destroyed all the world, and eight persons only escaped the angry baptism of water, and yet this world is the time of mercy; God hath opened here His magazines, and sent His Holy Son as the great channel and fountain of it, too: here He delights in mercy, and in judgment loves to remember it, and it triumphs over all His works, and God contrives instruments and accidents, chances and designs, occasions and opportunities for mercy. If, therefore, now the anger of God makes such terrible eruptions upon the wicked people that delight in sin, how great may we suppose that anger to be, how severe that judgment, how terrible that vengeance, how intolerable those inflictions which God reserves for the full effusion of indignation on the great day of vengeance!

We may also guess at it by this: if God upon all single instances, and in the midst of our sins, before they are come to the full, and sometimes in the beginning of an evil habit, be so fierce in His anger, what can we imagine it to be in that day when the wicked are to drink the dregs of that horrid potion, and count over all the particulars of their whole treasure of wrath? "This is the day of wrath, and God shall reveal, or bring forth, His righteous judgments." The expression is taken from Deut. xxxii., 34: "Is not this laid up in store with me, and sealed up among my treasures? I will restore it in the day of vengeance, for the Lord shall judge His people, and repent Himself for His servants." For so did the Lybian lion that was brought up under discipline, and taught to endure blows, and eat the meat of order and regular provision, and to suffer gentle usages and the familiarities of societies; but once He brake out into His own wildness, and killed two Roman boys; but those that forage in the Lybian mountains tread down and devour all that they meet or master; and when they have fasted two days, lay up an anger great as is their appetite, and bring certain death to all that can be overcome. God is pleased to compare himself to a lion; and though in this life He hath confined Himself with promises and gracious emanations of an infinite goodness, and limits himself by conditions and covenants, and suffers Himself to be overcome by prayers, and Himself hath invented ways of atonement and expiation; yet when He is provoked by our unhandsome and unworthy actions, He makes sudden breaches, and tears some of us in pieces, and of others He breaks their bones or affrights their hopes and secular gaieties, and fills their house with mourning and cypress, and groans and death. But when this Lion of the tribe of Judah shall appear upon His own mountain, the mountain of the Lord, in His natural dress of majesty, and that justice shall have her chain and golden fetters taken off, then justice shall strike, and mercy shall hold her hands; she shall strike sore strokes, and pity shall not break the blow; and God shall account with us by minutes, and for words, and for thoughts, and then He shall be severe to mark what is done amiss; and that justice may reign entirely, God shall open the wicked man's treasure, and tell the sums, and weigh grains and scruples. Said Philo upon the place of Deuteronomy before quoted: As there are treasures of good things, and God has crowns and scepters in store for His saints and servants, and coronets for martyrs, and rosaries for virgins, and vials full of prayers, and bottles full of tears, and a register of sighs and penitential groans, so God hath a treasure of wrath and fury, of scourges and scorpions, and then shall be produced the shame of lust, and the malice of envy, and the groans of the opprest, and the persecutions of the saints, and the cares of covetousness, and the troubles of ambition, and the insolencies of traitors, and the violence of rebels, and the rage of anger, and the uneasiness of impatience, and the restlessness of unlawful desires; and by this time the monsters and diseases will be numerous and intolerable, when God's heavy hand shall press the *sanies* and the intolerableness, the obliquity and the unreasonableness, the amazement and the disorder, the smart and the sorrow, the guilt and the punishment, out from all our sins, and pour them into one chalice, and mingle them with an infinite wrath, and make the wicked drink of all the vengeance, and force it down their unwilling throats with the violence of devils and accurst spirits.

We may guess at the severity of the Judge by the lesser strokes of that judgment which He is pleased to send upon sinners in this world, to make them afraid of the horrible pains of doomsday—I mean the torments of an unquiet conscience, the amazement and confusions of some sins and some persons. For I have sometimes seen persons surprised in a base action, and taken in the circumstances of crafty theft and secret injustices, before their excuse was ready. They have changed their color, their speech hath faltered, their tongue stammered, their eyes did wander and fix nowhere, till shame made them sink into their hollow eye-pits to retreat from the images and circumstances of discovery; their wits are lost, their reason useless, the whole order of their soul is decomposed, and they neither see, nor feel, nor think, as they used to do, but they are broken into disorder by a stroke of damnation and a lesser stripe of hell; but then if you come to observe a guilty and a base murderer, a condemned traitor, and see him harassed first by an evil conscience, and then pulled in pieces by the hangman's hooks, or broken upon sorrows and the wheel, we may then guess (as well as we can in this life) what the pains of that day shall be to accurst souls. But those we shall consider afterward in their proper scene; now only we are to estimate the severity of our Judge by the intolerableness of an evil conscience; if guilt will make a man despair—and despair will make a man mad, confounded, and dissolved in all the regions of his senses and more noble faculties, that he shall neither feel, nor hear, nor see anything but specters and illusions, devils and frightful dreams, and hear noises, and shriek fearfully, and look pale and distracted, like a hopeless man from the horrors and confusions of a lost battle, upon which all his hopes did stand—then the wicked must at the day of judgment expect strange things and fearful, and such which now no language can express, and then no patience can endure. Then only it can truly be said that he is inflexible and inexorable. No prayers then can move Him, no groans can cause Him to pity thee; therefore pity thyself in time, that when the Judge comes thou mayest be one of the sons of everlasting mercy, to whom pity belongs as part of thine inheritance, for all else shall without any remorse (except His own) be condemned by the horrible sentence.

That all may think themselves concerned in this consideration, let us remember that even the righteous and most innocent shall pass through a severe trial. Many of the ancients explicated this severity by the fire of conflagration, which say they shall purify those souls at the day of judgment, which in this life have built upon the foundation (hay and stubble) works of folly and false opinions, states of imperfection. So St. Augustine's doctrine was: "The great fire at doomsday shall throw some into the portion of the left hand, and others shall be purified and represented on the right." And the same is affirmed by Origen and Lactantius; and St. Hilary thus expostulates: "Since we are to give account for every idle word, shall we long for the day of judgment, wherein we must, every one of us, pass that unwearied fire in which those grievous punishments for expiating the soul from sins must be endured; for to such as have been baptized with the Holy Ghost it remaineth that they be consummated with the fire of judgment." And St. Ambrose adds: "That if any be as Peter or as John, they are baptized with this fire, and he that is purged here had need to be purged there again. Let him also purify us, that every one of us being burned with that flaming sword, not burned up or consumed, we may enter into Paradise, and give thanks unto the Lord who hath brought us into a place of refreshment." This opinion of theirs is, in the main of it, very uncertain; relying upon the sense of some obscure place of Scripture is only apt to represent the great severity of the Judge at that day, and it hath in it this only certainty, that even the most innocent person hath great need of mercy, and he that hath the greatest cause of confidence, altho he runs to no rocks to hide him, yet he runs to the protection of the cross, and hides himself under the shadow of the divine mercies: and he that shall receive the absolution of the blest sentence shall also suffer the terrors of the day, and the fearful circumstances of Christ's coming. The effect of this consideration is this: That if the righteous scarcely be saved, where shall the wicked and the sinner appear? And if St. Paul, whose conscience accused him not, yet durst not be too confident, because he was not hereby justified, but might be found faulty by the severer judgment of his Lord, how shall we appear, with all our crimes and evil habits round about us? If there be need of much mercy to the servants and friends of the Judge, then His enemies shall not be able to stand upright in judgment.

Let us next consider the circumstances of our appearing and his sentence; and first I consider that men at the day of judgment that belong not to the portion of life, shall have three sorts of accusers: 1. Christ Himself, who is their judge; 2. Their own conscience, whom they have injured and blotted with characters of death and foul dishonor; 3. The devil, their enemy, whom they served.

Christ shall be their accuser, not only upon the stock of those direct injuries (which I before reckoned) of crucifying the Lord of Life, once and again, etc., but upon the titles of contempt and unworthiness, of unkindness and ingratitude; and the accusation will be nothing else but a plain representation of those artifices and assistances, those bonds and invitations, those constrainings and importunities, which our dear Lord used to us to make it almost impossible to lie in sin, and necessary to be saved. For it will, it must needs be, a fearful exprobration of our unworthiness, when the Judge Himself shall bear witness against us that the wisdom of God Himself was strangely employed in bringing us safely to felicity. I shall draw a short scheme which, altho it must needs be infinitely short, of what God hath done for us, yet it will be enough to shame us. God did not only give His Son for an example, and the Son gave Himself for a price for us, but both gave the Holy Spirit to assist us in mighty graces, for the verifications of faith, and the entertainments of hope, and the increase and perseverance of charity. God gave to us a new nature, He put another principle into us, a third part of a perfective constitution; we have the spirit put into us, to be a part of us, as properly to produce actions of a holy life, as the soul of man in the body does produce the natural. God hath exalted human nature, and made it in the person of Jesus Christ, to sit above the highest seat of angels, and the angels are made ministering spirits, ever since their Lord became our brother. Christ hath by a miraculous sacrament given us His body to eat and His blood to drink; He made ways that we may become all one with Him. He hath given us an easy religion, and hath established our future felicity upon natural and pleasant conditions, and we are to be happy hereafter if we suffer God to make us happy here; and things are so ordered that a man must take more pains to perish than to be happy. God hath found out rare ways to make our prayers acceptable, our weak petitions, the desires of our imperfect souls, to prevail mightily with God, and to lay a holy violence and an undeniable necessity upon Himself; and God will deny us nothing but when we ask of Him to do us ill offices, to give us poisons and dangers, and evil nourishment, and temptations; and He that hath given such mighty power to the prayers of His servants, yet will not be moved by those potent and mighty prayers to do any good man an evil turn, or to grant him one mischief—in that only God can deny us. But in all things else God hath made all the excellent things in heaven and earth to join toward the holy and fortunate effects; for He that appointed an angel to present the prayers of saints, and Christ makes intercession for us, and the Holy Spirit makes intercession for us with groans unutterable, and all the holy men in the world pray for all and for every one, and God hath instructed us with scriptures, and precedents, and collateral and direct assistances to pray, and He encouraged us with divers excellent promises, and parables, and examples, and teaches us what to pray, and how, and gives one promise to public prayer, and another to private prayer, and to both the blessing of being heard.

Add to this account that God did heap blessings upon us without order, infinitely, perpetually, and in all instances, when we needed and when we needed not. He heard us when we prayed, giving us all, and giving us more, than we desired. He desired that we should ask, and yet He hath also prevented our desires. He watched for us, and at His own charge sent a whole order of men whose employment is to minister to our souls; and if all this had not been enough, He had given us more also. He promised heaven to our obedience, a province for a dish of water, a kingdom for a prayer, satisfaction for desiring it, grace for receiving, and more grace for accepting and using the first. He invited us with gracious words and perfect entertainments; He threatened horrible things to us if we would not be happy; He hath made strange necessities for us, making our very repentance to be a conjugation of holy actions, and holy times, and a long succession; He hath taken away all excuses from us; He hath called us from temptation; He bears our charges; He is always beforehand with us in every act of favor, and perpetually slow in striking, and His arrows are unfeathered; and He is so long, first, in drawing His sword, and another long while in whetting it, and yet longer in lifting His hand to strike, that before the blow comes the man hath repented long, unless he be a fool and impudent; and then God is so glad of an excuse to lay His anger aside, that certainly, if after all this, we refuse life and glory, there is no more to be said; this plain story will condemn us; but the story is very much longer; and, as our conscience will represent all our sins to us, so the Judge will represent all His Father's kindnesses, as Nathan did to David, when he was to make the justice of the divine sentence appear against him. Then it shall be remembered that the joys of every day's piety would have been a greater pleasure every night than the remembrance of every night's sin could have been in the morning; that every night the trouble and labor of the day's virtue would have been as much passed and turned to as the pleasure of that day's sin, but that they would be infinitely distinguished by the effects. The offering ourselves to God every morning, and the thanksgiving to God every night, hope and fear, shame and desire, the honor of leaving a fair name behind us, and the shame of dying like a fool,—everything indeed in the world is made to be an argument and an inducement to us to invite us to come to God and be saved; and therefore when this, and infinitely more shall by the Judge be exhibited in sad remembrances, there needs no other sentence; we shall condemn ourselves with a hasty shame and a fearful confusion, to see how good God hath been to us, and how base we have been to ourselves. Thus Moses is said to accuse the

Jews; and thus also He that does accuse, is said to condemn, as Verres was by Cicero, and Claudia by Domitius her accuser, and the world of impenitent persons by the men of Nineveh, and all by Christ, their Judge. I represent the horror of this circumstance to consist in this, besides the reasonableness of the judgment, and the certainty of the condemnation, it can not but be an argument of an intolerable despair to perishing souls, when He that was our advocate all our life, shall, in the day of that appearing, be our Accuser and our Judge, a party against us, an injured person in the day of His power and of His wrath, doing execution upon all His own foolish and malicious enemies.

Our conscience shall be our accuser. But this signifies but these two things: First, That we shall be condemned for the evils that we have done and shall then remember, God by His power wiping away the dust from the tables of our memory, and taking off the consideration and the voluntary neglect and rude shufflings of our cases of conscience. For then we shall see things as they are, the evil circumstances and the crooked intentions, the adherent unhandsomeness and the direct crimes; for all things are laid up safely, and tho we draw a curtain of cobweb over them, and a few fig-leaves before our shame, yet God shall draw away the curtain, and forgetfulness shall be no more, because, with a taper in the hand of God, all the corners of our nastiness shall be discovered. And, secondly, it signifies this also, that not only the justice of God shall be confest by us in our own shame and condemnation, but the evil of the sentence shall be received into us, to melt our bowels and to break our heart in pieces within us, because we are the authors of our own death, and our own inhuman hands have torn our souls in pieces. Thus far the horrors are great, and when evil men consider it, it is certain they must be afraid to die. Even they that have lived well, have some sad considerations, and the tremblings of humility, and suspicion of themselves. I remember St. Cyprian tells of a good man who in his agony of death saw a fantasm of a noble and angelical shape, who, frowning and angry, said to him: "Ye can not endure sickness, ye are troubled

45

at the evils of the world, and yet you are loath to die and to be quit of them; what shall I do to you?" Altho this is apt to represent every man's condition more or less, yet, concerning persons of wicked lives, it hath in it too many sad degrees of truth; they are impatient of sorrow, and justly fearful of death, because they know not how to comfort themselves in the evil accidents of their lives; and their conscience is too polluted to take death for sanctuary, and to hope to have amends made to their condition by the sentence of the day of judgment. Evil and sad is their condition who can not be contented here nor blest hereafter, whose life is their misery and their conscience is their enemy, whose grave is their prison and death their undoing, and the sentence of doomsday the beginning of an intolerable condition.

The third sort of accusers are the devils, and they will do it with malicious and evil purposes. The prince of the devils hath Diabolus for one of his chiefest appellatives. The accuser of the brethren he is by his profest malice and employment; and therefore God, who delights that His mercy should triumph and His goodness prevail over all the malice of men and devils, hath appointed one whose office is to reprove the accuser and to resist the enemy, and to be a defender of their cause who belong to God. The Holy Spirit is a defender; the evil spirit is the accuser; and they that in this life belong to one or the other, shall in the same proportion be treated at the day of judgment. The devil shall accuse the brethren, that is, the saints and servants of God, and shall tell concerning their follies and infirmities, the sins of their youth and weakness of their age, the imperfect grace and the long schedule of omissions of duty, their scruples and their fears, their diffidences and pusillanimity, and all those things which themselves by strict examination find themselves guilty of and have confest all their shame and the matter of their sorrows, their evil intentions and their little plots, their carnal confidences and too fond adherences of the things of this world, their indulgence and easiness of government, their wilder joys and freer meals, their loss of time and their too forward and apt compliances, their trifling arrests and little peevishnesses, the mixtures of the world with the thing of the Spirit, and all the incidences of humanity he will bring forth and aggravate them by circumstances of ingratitude, and the breach of promise, and the evacuating all their holy purposes, and breaking their resolutions, and rifling their vows, and all these things, being drawn into an entire representment, and the bills clogged by numbers, will make the best man in the world seem foul and unhandsome, and stained with the characters of death and evil dishonor. But for these there is appointed a defender. The Holy Spirit that maketh intercession for us shall then also interpose, and against all these things shall oppose the passion of our blest Lord, and upon all their defects shall cast the robe of righteousness; and the sins of their youth shall not prevail so much as the repentance of their age, and their omissions be excused by probable intervening causes, and their little escapes shall appear single and in disunion, because they were always kept asunder by penitential prayers and sighings, and their seldom returns of sin by their daily watchfulness, and their often infirmities by the sincerity of their souls, and their scruples by their zeal, and their passions by their love, and all by the mercies of God and the sacrifice which their Judge offered and the Holy Spirit made effective by daily graces and assistances. These, therefore, infallibly go to the portion of the right hand, because the Lord our God shall answer for them. But as for the wicked, it is not so with them; for altho the plain story of their life be to them a sad condemnation, yet what will be answered when it shall be told concerning them, that they despised God's mercies, and feared not His angry judgments; that they regarded not His Word, and loved not His excellences; that they were not persuaded by the promises nor affrighted by His threatenings; that they neither would accept His government nor His blessings; that all the sad stories that ever happened in both the worlds (in all which Himself did escape till the day of His death, and was not concerned in them save only that He was called upon by every one of them, which He ever heard or saw or was told of, to repentance), that all these were sent to Him in vain? But can not the accuser truly say to the Judge concerning such persons, "They were Thine by creation, but mine by their own choice; Thou didst redeem them indeed, but they sold themselves to me for a trifle, or for an unsatisfying interest; Thou diedst for them, but they obeyed my commandments; I gave them nothing, I promised them nothing but the filthy pleasures of a night, or the joys of madness, or the delights of a disease; I never hanged upon the cross three long hours for them, nor endured the labors of a poor life thirty-three years together for their interest; only when they were Thine by the merit of Thy death, they quickly became mine by the demerit of their ingratitude; and when Thou hadst clothed their soul with Thy robe, and adorned them by Thy graces, we stript them naked as their shame, and only put on a robe of darkness, and they thought themselves secure and went dancing to their grave like a drunkard to a fight, or a fly unto a candle; and therefore they that did partake with us in our faults must divide with us in our portion and fearful interest." This is a sad story because it ends in death, and there is nothing to abate or lessen the calamity. It concerns us therefore to consider in time that he that tempts us will accuse us, and what he calls pleasant now he shall then say was nothing, and all the gains that now invite earthly souls and mean persons to vanity, was nothing but the seeds of folly, and the harvest in pain and sorrow and shame eternal. But then, since this horror proceeds upon the account of so many accusers, God hath put it in our power by a timely accusation of ourselves in the tribunal of the court Christian, to prevent all the arts of aggravation which at doomsday shall load foolish and undiscerning souls. He that accuses himself of his crimes here, means to forsake them, and looks upon them on all sides, and spies out his deformity, and is taught to hate them, he is instructed and prayed for, he prevents the anger of God and defeats the devil's malice, and, by making shame the instrument of repentance, he takes away the sting, and makes that to be his medicine which otherwise would be his death: and, concerning this exercise, I shall only add what the patriarch of Alexandria told an old religious person in his hermitage. Having asked him what he found in that desert, he was answered, "Only this, to judge and condemn myself perpetually; that is the employment of my solitude." The patriarch answered, "There is no other way." By accusing ourselves we shall make the devil's malice useless, and our own consciences clear, and be reconciled to the Judge by the severities of an early repentance, and then we need to fear no accusers.

BAXTER

MAKING LIGHT OF CHRIST AND SALVATION

BIOGRAPHICAL NOTE

Richard Baxter, was born in 1615, at Rowton, near Shrewsbury, in England. After surmounting great difficulties in securing an education for the ministry he was ordained in 1638, in the Church of England, his first important charge being that of Kidderminster, where he established his reputation as a powerful evangelical and controversial preacher. Altho opposed to Cromwell's extreme acts, he became a chaplain in the army of the Rebellion. His influence was all on the side of peace, however, and at the Restoration he was appointed chaplain to Charles II.

Baxter left the Church of England on the promulgation of the Act of Uniformity, and in 1662 retired to Acton in Middlesex, where he wrote most of his works. The Acts of Indulgence enabled him to return to London, where he remained until Judge Jeffreys imprisoned and fined him on a charge of sedition. He was the most prolific writer and controversialist of his day among nonconformists. Baxter left only two works which seem likely to be of ever fresh interest, "The Saint's Rest" and "Calls to the Unconverted." He died in London in 1691.

BAXTER

1615-1691
MAKING LIGHT
OF CHRIST AND SALVATION

But they made light of it.—Matt, xxii., 5.

Beloved hearers; the office that God hath called us to is, by declaring the glory of His grace, to help under Christ to the saving of men's souls. I hope you think not that I come hither to-day on another errand. The Lord knows I had not set a foot out-of-doors but in hope to succeed in this work for your souls. I have considered, and often considered, what is the matter that so many thousands should perish when God hath done so much for their salvation; and I find this that is mentioned in my text is the cause. It is one of the wonders of the world, that when God hath so loved the world as to send His Son, and Christ hath made a satisfaction by His death sufficient for them all, and offereth the benefits of it so freely to them, even without money or price, that yet the most of the world should perish; yea, the most of those that are thus called by His Word! Why, here is the reason— when Christ hath done all this, men make light of it. God hath showed that He is not unwilling; and Christ hath showed that He is not unwilling that men should be restored to God's favor and be saved; but men are actually unwilling themselves. God takes not pleasure in the death of sinners, but rather that they return and live. But men take such pleasure in sin that they will die before they will return. The Lord Jesus was content to be their physician, and hath provided them a sufficient plaster of His own blood: but if men make light of it, and will not apply it, what wonder if they perish after all? This Scripture giveth us the reason of their perdition. This, sad experience tells us, the most of the world is guilty of. It is a most lamentable thing to see how most men do spend their care, their time, their pains, for known vanities, while God and glory are cast aside; that He who is all should seem to them as nothing, and that which is nothing should seem to them as good as all; that God should set mankind in such a race where heaven or hell is their certain end, and that they should sit down, and loiter, or run after the childish toys of the world, and so much forget the prize that they should run for. Were it but possible for one of us to see the whole of this business as the all-seeing God doth; to see at one view both heaven and hell, which men are so near; and see what most men in the world are minding, and what they are doing every day, it would be the saddest sight that could be imagined. Oh, how should we marvel at their madness, and lament their self-delusion! O poor distracted world! what is it you run after? and what is it that you neglect? If God had never told them what they were sent into the world to do, or whither they were going, or what was before them in another world, then they had been excusable; but He hath told them over and over, till they were weary of it. Had He left it doubtful, there had been some excuse; but it is His sealed word, and they profess to believe it, and would take it ill of us if we should question whether they do believe it or not.

Beloved, I come not to accuse any of you particularly of this crime; but seeing it is the commonest cause of men's destruction, I suppose you will judge it the fittest matter for our inquiry, and deserving our greatest care for the cure. To which end I shall, (1) endeavor the conviction of the guilty; (2) shall give them such considerations as may tend to humble and reform them; (3) I shall conclude with such direction as may help them that are willing to escape the destroying power of this sin.

And for the first, consider: It is the case of most sinners to think themselves freest from those sins that they are most enslaved to; and one reason why we can not reform them is because we can not convince them of their guilt. It is the nature of sin so far to blind and befool the sinner, that he knoweth not what he doth, but thinketh he is free from it when it reigneth in him, or when he is committing it: it bringeth men to be so much unacquainted with themselves that they know not what they think, or what they mean and intend, nor what they love or hate, much less what they are habituated and disposed to. They are alive to sin, and dead to all the reason, consideration, and resolution that should recover them, as if it were only by their sinning that we must know that they are alive. May I hope that you that hear me to-day are but willing to know the truth of your case, and then I shall be encouraged to proceed to an inquiry. God will judge impartially; why should not we do so? Let me, therefore, by these following questions, try whether none of you are slighters of Christ and your own salvation. And follow me, I beseech you, by putting them close to your own hearts, and faithfully answering them.

Things that men highly value will be remembered; they will be matter of their freest and sweetest thoughts. This is a known case.

Do not those then make light of Christ and salvation that think of them so seldom and coldly in comparison of other things? Follow thy own heart, man, and observe what it daily runneth after; and then judge whether it make not light of Christ.

We can not persuade men to one hour's sober consideration what they should do for an interest in Christ, or in thankfulness for His love, and yet they will not believe that they make light of Him.

Things that we highly value will be matter of our discourse; the judgment and heart will command the tongue. Freely and delightfully will our speech run after them. This also is a known case.

Do not those men make light of Christ and salvation that shun the mention of His name, unless it be in a vain or sinful use? Those that love not the company where Christ and salvation is much talked of, but think it troublesome, precise discourse:

that had rather hear some merry jests, or idle tales, or talk of their riches or business in the world; when you may follow them from morning to night, and scarce have a savory word of Christ; but perhaps some slight and weary mention of Him sometimes; judge whether these make not light of Christ and salvation. How seriously do they talk of the world and speak of vanity! but how heartlessly do they make mention of Christ and salvation!

The things that we highly value we would secure the possession of, and therefore would take any convenient course to have all doubts and fears about them well resolved. Do not those men then make light of Christ and salvation that have lived twenty or thirty years in uncertainty whether they have any part in these or not, and yet never seek out for the right resolution of their doubts? Are all that hear me this day certain they shall be saved? Oh, that they were! Oh, had you not made light of salvation, you could not so easily bear such doubting of it; you could not rest till you had made it sure, or done your best to make it sure. Have you nobody to inquire of, that might help you in such a work? Why, you have ministers that are purposely appointed to that office. Have you gone to them, and told them the doubtfulness of your case, and asked their help in the judging of your condition? Alas! ministers may sit in their studies from one year to another, before ten persons among a thousand will come to them on such an errand! Do not these make light of Christ and salvation? When the gospel pierceth the heart indeed, they cry out, "Men and brethren, what shall we do to be saved?" Trembling and astonished, Paul cries out, "Lord, what wilt Thou have me to do?" And so did the convinced Jews to Peter. But when hear we such questions?

The things that we value do deeply affect us, and some motions will be in the heart according to our estimation of them. O sirs, if men made not light of these things, what working would there be in the hearts of all our hearers! What strange affections would it raise in them to hear of the matters of the world to come! How would their hearts melt before the power of the gospel!

What sorrow would be wrought in the discovery of their sins! What astonishment at the consideration of their misery! What unspeakable joy at the glad tidings of salvation by the blood of Christ! What resolution would be raised in them upon the discovery of their duty! Oh, what hearers should we have, if it were not for this sin! Whereas now we are liker to weary them, or preach them asleep with matters of this unspeakable moment. We talk to them of Christ and salvation till we make their heads ache: little would one think by their careless carriage that they heard and regarded what we said, or tho we spoke at all to them.

Our estimation of things will be seen in the diligence of our endeavors. That which we highliest value, we shall think no pains too great to obtain. Do not those men then make light of Christ and salvation that think all too much that they do for them; that murmur at His service, and think it too grievous for them to endure? that ask His service as Judas of the ointment. What need this waste? Can not men be saved without so much ado? This is more ado than needs. For the world they will labor all the day, and all their lives; but for Christ and salvation they are afraid of doing too much. Let us preach to them as long as we will, we can not bring them to relish or resolve upon a life of holiness. Follow them to their houses, and you shall not hear them read a chapter, nor call upon God with their families once a day; nor will they allow Him that one day in seven which He hath separated to His service. But pleasure, or worldly business, or idleness, must have a part And many of them are so far hardened as to reproach them that will not be as mad as themselves. And is not Christ worth the seeking? Is not everlasting salvation worth more than all this? Doth not that soul make light of all these that thinks his ease more worth than they? Let but common sense judge.

That which we most highly value, we think we can not buy too dear. Christ and salvation are freely given, and yet the most of men go without them because they can not enjoy the world and them together. They are called but to part with that which would hinder them Christ, and they will not do it. They are called but to give God His own, and to resign all to His will, and let go the profits and pleasures of this world, when they must let go either Christ or them, and they will not. They think this too dear a bargain, and say they can not spare these things: they must hold their credit with men; they must look to their estates: how shall they live else? They must have their pleasure, whatsoever becomes of Christ and salvation: as if they could live without Christ better than without these; as if they were afraid of being losers by Christ, or could make a saving match by losing their souls to gain the world. Christ hath told us over and over that if we will not forsake all for Him we can not be His disciples. Far are these men from forsaking all, and yet will needs think that they are His disciples indeed.

That which men highly esteem, they would help their friends to as well as themselves. Do not those men make light of Christ and salvation that can take so much care to leave their children portions in the world, and do so little to help them to heaven? that provide outward necessaries so carefully for their families, but do so little to the saving of their souls? Their neglected children and friends will witness that either Christ, or their children's souls, or both, were made light of.

That which men highly esteem, they will so diligently seek after that you may see it in the success, if it be a matter within their reach. You may see how many make light of Christ, by the little knowledge they have of Him, and the little communion with Him, and the communication from Him; and the little, yea, none, of His special grace in them. Alas! how many ministers can speak it to the sorrow of their hearts, that many of their people know almost nothing of Christ, tho they hear of Him daily! Nor know they what they must do to be saved: if we ask them an account of these things, they answer as if they understood not what we say to them, and tell us they are no scholars, and therefore think they are excusable for their ignorance. Oh, if these men had not made light of Christ and their salvation, but had bestowed but half as much pains to know and enjoy Him as they have done to understand the matters of their trades and callings in the world, they would not have been so ignorant as they are: they make light of these things, and therefore will not be at the pains to study or learn them. When men that can learn the hardest trade in a few years have not learned a catechism, nor how to understand their creed, under twenty or thirty years' preaching, nor can abide to be questioned about such things, doth not this show that they have slighted them in their hearts? How will these despisers of Christ and salvation be able one day to look Him in the face, and to give an account of these neglects?

Thus much I have spoken in order to your conviction. Do not some of your consciences by this time smite you, and say, I am the man that have made light of my salvation? If they do not, it is because you make light of it still, for all that is said to you. But because, if it be the will of the Lord, I would fain have this damning distemper cured, and am loath to leave you in such a desperate condition, if I knew how to remedy it, I will give you some considerations, which may move you, if you be men of reason and understanding, to look better about you; and I beseech you to weigh them, and make use of them as we go, and lay open your hearts to the work of grace, and sadly bethink you what a case you are in, if you prove such as make light of Christ.

Consider, 1. Thou makest light of Him that made not light of thee who deserve it. Thou wast worthy of nothing but contempt. As a man, what art thou but a worm to God? As a sinner, thou art far viler than a toad: yet Christ was so far from making light of thee and thy happiness, that He came down into the flesh, and lived a life of suffering, and offered Himself a sacrifice to the justice which thou hadst provoked, that thy miserable soul might have a remedy. It is no less than miracles of love and mercy that He hath showed to us; and yet shall we slight them after all?

Angels admire them, whom they less concern, and shall redeemed sinners make light of them? What barbarous, yea, devilish—yea, worse than devilish—ingratitude is this! The devils never had a savior offered to them; but thou hast, and dost thou yet make light of Him?

2. Consider, the work of man's salvation by Jesus Christ is the masterpiece of all the works of God, wherein He would have His love and mercy to be magnified. As the creation declareth. His goodness and power, so doth redemption His goodness and mercy; He hath contrived the very frame of His worship so that it shall much consist in the magnifying of this work; and, after all this, will you make light of it? "His name is wonderful." "He did the work that none could do." "Greater love could none show than His." How great was the evil and misery that He delivered us from! the good procured from us! All are wonders, from His birth to His ascension; from our new birth to our glorification, all are wonders of matchless mercy—and yet do you make light of them?

3. You make light of matters of greatest excellency and moment in the world: you know not what it is that you slight: had you well known, you would not have done it. As Christ said to the woman of Samaria, "Hadst thou known who it is that speaketh to thee, thou wouldst have asked of Him the waters of life"; had they known they would not have crucified the Lord of Glory. So, had you known what Christ is, you would not have made light of Him; had you been one day in heaven, and but seen what they possess, and seen also what miserable souls must endure that are shut out, you would never sure have made so light of Christ.

O sirs, it is no trifles or jesting matters that the gospel speaks of. I must needs profess to you that when I have the most serious thoughts of these things myself, I am ready to marvel that such amazing matters do not overwhelm the souls of men; that the greatness of the subject doth not so overmatch our understandings and affections as even to drive men besides themselves, but that God hath always somewhat allayed it by the distance; much more that men should be so blockish as to make light of them. O Lord, that men did but know what everlasting glory and everlasting torments are: would they then hear us as they do? would they read and think of these things as they do? I profess I have been ready to wonder, when I have heard such weighty things delivered, how people can forbear crying out in the congregation; much more how they can rest till they have gone to their ministers, and learned what they should do to be saved, that this great business might be put out of doubt. Oh, that heaven and hell should work no more on men! Oh, that everlastingness work no more! Oh, how can you forbear when you are alone to think with yourselves what it is to be everlastingly in joy or in torment! I wonder that such thoughts do not break your sleep, and that they come not in your mind when you are about your labor! I wonder how you can almost do anything else! how you can have any quietness in your minds! How you can eat, or drink, or rest, till you have got some ground of everlasting consolations! Is that a man or a corpse that is not affected with matters of this moment? that can be readier to sleep than to tremble when he heareth how he must stand at the bar of God? Is that a man or a clod of clay that can rise or lie down without being deeply affected with his everlasting estate? that can follow his worldly business and make nothing of the great business of salvation or damnation; and that when they know it is hard at hand? Truly, sirs, when I think of the weight of the matter, I wonder at the very best of God's saints upon the earth that they are no better, and do no more in so weighty a case. I wonder at those whom the world accounteth more holy than needs, and scorns for making too much ado, that they can put off Christ and their souls with so little; that they pour not out their souls in every supplication; that they are not more taken up with God; that their thoughts be more serious in preparation for their account. I wonder that they be not a hundred times more strict in their lives, and more laborious and unwearied in striving for the crown, than they are. And for myself, as I am ashamed of my dull and careless heart, and of my slow and unprofitable course of life, so the Lord knows I am ashamed of every sermon that I preach: when I think what I have been speaking of, and who sent me, and that men's salvation or damnation is so much concerned in it, I am ready to tremble lest God should judge me as a slighter of His truth and the souls of men, and lest in the best sermon I should be guilty of their blood. Methinks we should not speak a word to men in matters of such consequence without tears, or the greatest earnestness that possibly we can: were not we too much guilty of the sin which we reprove, it would be so. Whether we are alone, or in company, methinks our end, and such an end, should still be in our mind, and before our eyes; and we should sooner forget anything, and set light by anything, or by all things, than by this.

Consider, 4. Who is it that sends this weighty message to you? Is it not God Himself? Shall the God of heaven speak and men make light of it? You would not slight the voice of an angel or a prince.

5. Whose salvation is it that you make light of? Is it not your own? Are you no more near or dear to yourselves than to make light of your own happiness or misery? Why, sirs, do you not care whether you be saved or damned? Is self-love lost? are you turned your own enemies? As he that slighteth his meat doth slight his life, so if you slight Christ, whatsoever you may think, you will find it was your own salvation that you slighted. Hear what He saith, "All they that hate me love death."

6. Your sin is greater, in that you profess to believe the gospel which you make so light of. For a profest infidel to do it that believes not that ever Christ died, or rose again, or doth not believe that there is a heaven or hell, this were no such marvel— but for you, that make it your creed, and your very religion, and call yourselves Christians, and have been baptized into this faith, and seemed to stand to it, this is the wonder, and hath no excuse. What! believe that you shall live in endless joy or torment, and yet make no more of it to escape torment, and obtain that joy! What! believe that God will shortly judge you, and yet make no preparation for it! Either say plainly, I am no Christian, I do not believe these wonderful things, I will believe nothing but what I see, or else let your hearts be affected with your belief, and live as

you say you do believe. What do you think when you repeat the creed, and mention Christ's judgment and everlasting life?

7. What are these things you set so much by as to prefer them before Christ and the saving of your soul? Have you found a better friend, a greater and a surer happiness than this? Good Lord! what dung is it that men make so much of, while they set so light by everlasting glory? What toys are they that are daily taken up with, while matters of life and death are neglected? Why, sirs, if you had every one a kingdom in your hopes, what were it in comparison of the everlasting kingdom? I can not but look upon all the glory and dignity of this world, lands and lordships, crowns and kingdoms, even as on some brain-sick, beggarly fellow, that borroweth fine clothes, and plays the part of a king or a lord for an hour on a stage, and then comes down, and the sport is ended, and they are beggars again. Were it not for God's interest in the authority of magistrates, or for the service they might do Him, I should judge no better of them. For, as to their own glory, it is but a smoke: what matter is it whether you live poor or rich, unless it were a greater matter to die rich than it is? You know well enough that death levels all. What matter is it at judgment, whether you be to answer for the life of a rich man or a poor man? Is Dives, then, any better than Lazarus? Oh, that men knew what poor, deceiving shadow they grasp at while they let go the everlasting substance! The strongest, and richest, and most voluptuous sinners do but lay in fuel for their sorrows, while they think they are gathering together a treasure. Alas! they are asleep, and dream that they are happy; but when they awake, what a change will they find! Their crown is made of thorns; their pleasure hath such a sting as will stick in the heart through all eternity, except unfeigned repentance do prevent it. Oh, how sadly will these wretches be convinced ere long, what a foolish bargain they made in selling Christ and their salvation for these trifles! Let your farms and merchandise, then, save you, if they can, and do that for you that Christ would have done. Cry then to Baal, to save thee! Oh, what thoughts have drunkards

and adulterers, etc., of Christ, that will not part with the basest lust for Him? "For a piece of bread," saith Solomon, "such men do transgress."

8. To set so light by Christ and salvation is a certain mark that thou hast no part in them, and if thou so continue, that Christ will set as light by thee: "Those that honor him he will honor, and those that despise him shall be lightly esteemed." Thou wilt feel one day that thou canst not live without Him; thou wilt confess then thy need of Him; and then thou mayest go look for a savior where thou wilt; for He will be no Savior for thee hereafter, that wouldst not value Him, and submit to Him here. Then who will prove the loser by thy contempt? Oh, what a thing will it be for a poor miserable soul to cry to Christ for help in the day of extremity, and to hear so sad an answer as this! Thou didst set lightly by Me and My law in the day of thy prosperity, and I will now set as light by thee in the day of thy adversity. Read Prov. i., 24, to the end. Thou that, as Esau, didst sell thy birthright for a mess of pottage, shalt then find no place for repentance, tho thou seek it with tears. Do you think that Christ shed His blood to save them that continue to make light of it? and to save them, that value a cup of drink or a lust before His salvation? I tell you, sirs, tho you set so light by Christ and salvation, God doth not so: He will not give them on such terms as these: He valueth the blood of His Son, and the everlasting glory, and He will make you value them if ever you have them. Nay, this will be thy condemnation, and leaveth no remedy. All the world can not save him that sets lightly by Christ. None of them shall taste of His supper. Nor can you blame Him to deny you what you made light of yourselves. Can you find fault if you miss of the salvation which you slighted?

9. The time is near when Christ and salvation will not be made light of as now they are. When God hath shaken those careless souls out of their bodies, and you must answer for all your sins in your own name, oh, then, what would you not give for a Savior! When a thousand bills shall be brought in against you, and

none to relieve you, then you will consider, Oh! Christ would now have stood between me and the wrath of God; had I not despised Him, He would have answered all. When you see the world hath left you, and your companions in sin have deceived themselves and you, and all your merry days are gone, then what would you not give for that Christ and salvation that now you account not worth your labor! Do you think that when you see the judgment seat, and you are doomed to everlasting perdition for your wickedness, that you should then make as light of Christ as now? Why will you not judge now as you know you shall judge then? Will He then be worth ten thousand worlds? And is He not now worth your highest estimation and dearest affection?

10. God will not only deny thee that salvation thou madest light of, but He will take from thee all that which thou didst value before it: he that most highly esteems Christ shall have Him, and the creatures, so far as they are good here, and Him without the creature hereafter, because the creature is not useful; and he that sets more by the creature than by Christ, shall have some of the creature without Christ here, and neither Christ nor it hereafter.

So much of these considerations, which may show the true face of this heinous sin.

What think you now, friends, of this business? Do you not see by this time what a case that soul is in that maketh light of Christ and salvation? What need then is there that you should take heed lest this should prove your own case! The Lord knows it is too common a case. Whoever is found guilty at the last of this sin, it were better for that man he had never been born. It were better for him he had been a Turk or Indian, that never had heard the name of a Savior, and that never had salvation offered to him: for such men "have no cloak for their sin." Besides all the rest of their sins, they have this killing sin to answer for, which will undo them. And this will aggravate their misery, that Christ whom they set light by must be their Judge, and for this sin will He judge them. Oh, that such would now consider how they will answer that question that Christ put to their predecessors: "How will ye escape the damnation of hell" or, "How shall we escape if we neglect so great salvation?" Can you escape without a Christ? or will a despised Christ save you then? If he be accurst that sets light by father or mother, what then is he that sets light by Christ? It was the heinous sin of the Jews, that among them were found such as set light by father and mother. But among us, men slight the Father of Spirits! In the name of God, brethren, I beseech you to consider how you will then bear this anger which you now make light of! You that can not make light of a little sickness or want, or of natural death, no, not of a toothache, but groan as if you were undone; how will you then make light of the fury of the Lord, which will burn against the contemners of His grace! Doth it not behoove you beforehand to think of these things?

Dearly beloved in the Lord, I have now done that work which I came upon; what effect it hath, or will have, upon your hearts, I know not, nor is it any further in my power to accomplish that which my soul desireth for you. Were it the Lord's will that I might have my wish herein, the words that you have this day heard should so stick by you that the secure should be awakened by them, and none of you should perish by the slighting of your salvation. I can not follow you to your several habitations to apply this word to your particular necessities; but oh, that I could make every man's conscience a preacher to himself that it might do it, which is ever with you! That the next time you go prayerless to bed, or about your business, conscience might cry out, Dost thou set no more by Christ and thy salvation? That the next time you are tempted to think hardly of a holy and diligent life (I will not say to deride it as more ado than needs), conscience might cry out to thee, Dost thou set so light by Christ and thy salvation? That the next time you are ready to rush upon unknown sin, and to please your fleshly desires against the command of God, conscience might cry out, Is Christ and salvation no more worth than to cast them away, or venture them for thy lust? That when you are following the world with your most eager desires, forgetting the world to come, and the change that is a little before you, conscience might cry out to you, Is Christ and salvation no more worth than so? That when you are next spending the Lord's day in idleness or vain sports, conscience might tell you what you are doing. In a word, that in all your neglects of duty, your sticking at the supposed labor or cost of a godly life, yea, in all your cold and lazy prayers and performances, conscience might tell you how unsuitable such endeavors are to the reward; and that Christ and salvation should not be so slighted. I will say no more but this at this time, it is a thousand pities that when God hath provided a Savior for the world, and when Christ hath suffered so much for their sins, and made so full a satisfaction to justice, and purchased so glorious a kingdom for His saints, and all this is offered so freely to sinners, to lost, unworthy sinners, even for nothing, that yet so many millions should everlastingly perish because they make light of their Savior and salvation, and prefer the vain world and their lusts before them. I have delivered my message, the Lord open your hearts to receive it. I have persuaded you with the word of truth and soberness; the Lord persuade you more effectually, or else all this is lost. Amen.

BOSSUET

THE FUNERAL SERMON
ON THE DEATH OF THE GRANDE CONDÉ

BIOGRAPHICAL NOTE

Jacque Benigne Bossuet was born at Dijon, in Burgundy, in 1627. In an illustrious group of French Catholic preachers he occupied a foremost place. In beginning his sermons he was reserved and dignified, but as he moved forward and his passionate utterance captured his hearers, "he watched their rising emotion, the rooted glances of a thousand eyes filled him with a sort of divine frenzy, his notes became a burden and a hindrance, and with impetuous ardor he abandoned himself to the inspiration of the moment."

To ripe scholarship Bossuet added a voice that was deep and sonorous, an imposing personality, and an animated and graceful style of gesture. Lamartine says he had "a voice which, like that of the thunder in the clouds, or the organ in the cathedral, had never been anything but the medium of power and divine persuasion to the soul; a voice which only spoke to kneeling auditors; a voice which spoke in the name of God, an authority of language unequaled upon earth, and against which the lowest murmur was impious and the smallest opposition blasphemy." He died in 1704.

BOSSUET

1627-1704
THE FUNERAL SERMON
ON THE DEATH OF THE GRANDE CONDÉ

In beginning this address, in which I purpose to celebrate
the immortal glory of Louis de Bourbon, Prince de Condé, I
feel myself overweighted both by the grandeur of the subject
and, to be frank, by the fruitlessness of the effort. What part of
the inhabited world has not heard of the victories of the Prince
de Condé and the wonders of his life? They are recounted
everywhere; the Frenchman who boasts of them in the presence
of the foreigner tells him nothing which the latter does not
know; and in no matter how exalted a strain I might sound his
praises, I should still feel that in your hearts you were convinced
that I deserved the reproach of falling far short of doing him
justice. An orator, feeble as he is, can not do anything for the
perpetuation of the glory of extraordinary souls. Le Sage was
right when he said that "their deeds alone can praise them"; no
other praise is of any effect where great names are concerned;
and it needs but the simple story of his deeds faithfully recorded
to sustain the glory of the Prince de Condé.

But, while awaiting the appearance of the history which is to
tell the story of his life to coming ages, it is necessary to satisfy
as best we may the public recognition of his merit and bow to
the order of the greatest of all sovereigns. What does not the
kingdom owe to a prince who has honored the house of France,
the French name, his century, and, so to speak, all mankind?
Louis the Great himself shares these sentiments; after having
mourned this great man, and by his tears, shed in the presence of

71

his entire court, rather than by words, uttered the most glorious eulogy he could receive, he assembled together in this celebrated temple all that is most august in his realm, in order that the last rites to the memory of this prince might there be celebrated; and he wishes that my feeble voice should animate all this funeral equipage. Let us try, then, to forget our grief. Here an object greater and worthier of this pulpit presents itself to my mind: it is God, who makes warriors and conquerors. "It is Thou," said David unto Him, "who hast trained my hand to battle, and my fingers to hold the sword." If He inspires courage, no less is He the bestower of other great qualities, both of heart and of mind. His mighty hand is the source of everything; it is He who sends from heaven generous sentiments, wise counsels and every worthy thought. But He wishes us to know how to distinguish between the gifts He abandons to His enemies and those He reserves for His servants. What distinguishes His friends from all others is piety. Until this gift of heaven has been received, all others not only are as naught, but even bring ruin on those who are endowed with them; without this inestimable gift of piety what would the Prince de Condé have been, even with his great heart and great genius? No, my brethren, if piety had not, as it were, consecrated his other virtues, these princes would have found no consolation for their grief, nor this pontiff any confidence in his prayers, nor would I myself utter with conviction the praises which I owe so great a man.

Let us, by this example, then set human glory at naught; let us destroy the idol of the ambitious, that it might fall to pieces before this altar. Let us to-day join together (for with a subject so noble we may do it) all the finest qualities of a superior nature; and, for the glory of truth, let us demonstrate, in a prince admired of the universe, that what makes heroes, that what carries to the highest pitch worldly glory, worth, magnanimity, natural goodness— all attributes of the heart; vivacity, penetration, grandeur and sublimity of genius—attributes of the mind; would be but an illusion were piety not a part of them—in a word, that piety is the essence of the man. It is this, gentlemen, which you will see in the forever memorable life of the most high and mighty Prince Louis de Bourbon, Prince de Condé, first prince of the blood.

God has revealed to us that He alone creates conquerors, and that He makes them serve His designs. What other created a Cyrus if it is not God, who named him two hundred years before his birth in the Prophecies of Isaiah? "Thou art as yet unborn," He said unto him, "but I see thee, and I named thee by thy name; thou shalt be called Cyrus. I will walk before thee in battle, at thy approach I will put kings to flight; I will break down doors of brass. It is I that stretch out the heavens, that support the earth, that name that which is not as that which is," that is to say, it is I that create everything and I that see, from eternity, all that I create. What other could fashion an Alexander, if it is not this same God who caused the unquenchable ardor of Daniel, His prophet, to see from so great a distance and by means of foreshadowings so vivid. "Do you see him," he says, "this conqueror; with what rapidity he rises from the west by bounds, as it were, and touches not the earth?"

In the boldness of his leaps, and the lightness of his tread like unto some powerful and frisking beast, he advances by quick and impetuous bounds, and nor mountain nor precipice arrests his progress. Already has the King of Persia fallen into his hands. "At his sight he was exasperated; *efferatus est in eum*," says the prophet; "he strikes him down, he tramples him under foot; none can save him from his blows nor cheat him of his prey." But to hear these words of Daniel, whom would you suppose you perceived, gentlemen, under that figure of speech— Alexander or the Prince de Condé? God gave him that dauntless valor that France might enjoy safety during the minority of a king but four years old. Let him grow up, this king, cherished of Heaven, and all will yield to his exploits; rising above his own followers, as well as his enemies, he will know how sometimes to make use of, and at others to dispense with, his most illustrious captains, and alone, under the hand of God, who will be his constant aid, he will be seen to be the stanch rampart of his dominions. But God chose the Duc d'Enghien to defend him in his infancy. So, toward the first days of his reign, at the age of twenty-two years, the duke conceived a plan in the armor of which the seasoned veterans could find no vulnerable point; but victory justified his course at Rocroi. The opposing force, it is true, is stronger; it is composed of those old Walloon, Italian and Spanish regiments that, up to that time, could not be broken; but at what valuation should be placed the courage inspired in our troops by the pressing necessities of the state, by past successes, and by a young prince of the blood in whose eyes could be read victory? Don Francisco de Mellos awaits the onset with a firm foot; and, without being able to retreat, the two generals and the two armies seemed to have wished to imprison themselves in the woods and the marshes in order to decide the issue of combat like two champions in the lists.

Then what a sight is presented to the eye! the young prince appears another man; touched by an object so worthy, his great soul displays all its sublimity; his courage waxes with the dangers it has to encounter, and his penetration becomes keener as his ardor increases. That night, which had to be spent in the presence of the enemy, like the vigilant commander that he was, he was the last to retire. But never were his slumbers more peaceful. On the eve of so momentous a day, when the first battle is to be fought, his mind is entirely tranquil, so thoroughly is he in his element; and it is well known that on the morrow, at the hour he had indicated, it was necessary to awaken this second Alexander from a deep slumber. Do you see him as he rushes on to victory or death? No sooner had he inspired the ranks with the ardor with which his soul was animated than he was seen almost at the same time to press the right wing of the enemy, support our own shaken by the shock of the charge, rally the disheartened and almost vanquished French forces, put to flight the victorious Spaniards, carrying dismay everywhere, and terrifying by his lightning glances those who escape his blows. There still remained that dreaded infantry of the Spanish army, whose great battalions in close line of battle like so many towers, but towers which knew how to repair their breaches, were unshaken by the onset, and, tho the rest of the army was put to rout, maintained a steady fire. Thrice the young conqueror attempted to break the ranks of these intrepid warriors, thrice was he repulsed by the valorous Comte de Fontaines, who was borne to the scene of combat in his invalid's chair, by reason of his bodily infirmities, thus demonstrating that the warrior's soul has the ascendant over the body it animates.

But at last was he forced to yield. In vain does Beck, with a body of fresh cavalry, hasten his march through the woods in order to attack our exhausted soldiers; the prince has forestalled him; the defeated battalions are asking quarter. But victory for the Duc d'Enghien was destined to be more terrible than the combat. While with an air of confidence he advances to receive the surrender of these brave fellows, they, on their part, still on their guard, are in dread of being surprized by a fresh attack. The frightful havoc wrought by the discharge of their musketry infuriates our troops. Carnage is now rampant; the bloodshed intoxicates the soldiers to a high degree. But the prince, who could not bear to see these lions slaughtered like so many lambs, calmed their overwrought feeling and enhanced the pleasure of victory by that of pardoning the vanquished. What, then, was the astonishment of these veteran troops and their brave officers when they perceived that their only salvation was to give themselves up to their conqueror! With what wonder did they regard the young prince, whose victory had rendered still more impressive his customary proud bearing, to which, however, his clemency had imparted a new grace. How willingly would he have saved the life of the brave Comte de Fontaines, but unhappily he lay stretched upon the field of battle among the thousands of dead bodies, those whose loss is still kept by Spain. Spain knew not that the prince who caused her the loss of so many of her old regiments on the day of Rocroi was to finish the rest on the plains of Lens.

Thus the first victory was the guarantee of many others. The prince bent his knee and on the field of battle rendered to the Lord of Hosts the glory He had sent him. There was celebrated the deliverance of Rocroi, and thanksgivings were uttered that the threats of a once dreaded enemy had resulted in his own shameful defeat; that the regency was strengthened, France calmed, and a reign which was to be so illustrious begun by an augury so auspicious. The army led in thanksgiving; all France followed; the first venture of the Duc d'Enghien was lauded to the skies. Praise sufficient to render others forever illustrious; but for him it was but the first stage in his career!

As a result of this first campaign, and after the capture of Thionville—a prize worthy of the victory gained at Rocroi—he was regarded as an adversary equally to be feared in sieges and in battles. But there is one trait in the character of the victorious young prince no less admirable than that which was brought out by victory. The court, which at his arrival was prepared to welcome him with the plaudits he deserved, was surprized at the manner in which he received them. The queen-regent assured him that the king was well pleased with his services. This from the lips of his sovereign was a fitting recompense for his labors. If others dared to praise him, however, he treated their eulogies as insults, and, impatient of flattery, he was in dread even of its semblance. Such was the delicacy, or rather the solidity of character, of this prince. Moreover his maxim was (listen, for it is a maxim which makes great men), that, in the performance of great deeds, one's sole thought should be to perform them well, and leave glory to follow in the train of virtue. It is this which he has endeavored to instil into others, and by this principle has he himself ever been guided. Thus false glory had no temptation for him. It was with truth and greatness alone that he was concerned.

Thus it came about that his glory was wrapt up in the service of his kind and in the happiness and well-being of the state; They were the objects nearest his heart; these were his first and most cherished desires. The court had but little charm for him, or occupation suited to his talents, tho he was there regarded as its greatest hero. It was deemed needful to exhibit everywhere in Germany, as in Flanders, the intrepid defender whom God had given us. Remark well what is about to transpire: There is being formed against the prince an enterprise of a more formidable nature than, that at Rocroi; and, in order to put his talents to the test, warfare is about to drain all its resources, and call to its aid every known invention. What is it that is presented to my vision? I see not merely men to meet in combat but inaccessible mountains: on one side are ravines and precipices; on the other impenetrable forests in the heart of which are marshes, and in proximity to streams are impregnable intrenchments; everywhere are lofty fortresses and forests of felled trees lying across roads which are frightful; and there arises Merci, with his worthy Bavarians inflated by the large measure of success which has fallen to their arms and by the capture of Fribourg; Merci, whom none has ever seen retreat from the combat; Merci, whom the Prince de Condé and the vigilant Turenne have never surprized in a movement that was not in accord with the rales of warfare, and to whom they have conceded this great mark of admiration—that never has he lost a single favorable opportunity, nor failed to anticipate their designs as tho he had taken part in their councils.

Here, then, in the course of eight days, and by four separate attacks, is seen how much can be supported and undertaken in war. Our troops seem as much dispirited by the frightful condition of the field of battle as by the resistance of the enemy, and for a time the prince sees himself, so to speak, abandoned. But like a second Maccabee, "his right arm abandons him not, and his courage, inflamed by so many perils, came to his aid." No sooner had he been seen on foot the first to scale those inaccessible heights, than his ardor drew the whole army after him. Merci sees himself lost beyond redemption; his best regiments are defeated; nightfall is the salvation of the remainder of his army. But a severe rainstorm serves to add to our difficulties and discouragements, so that we have at the same time to contend with not only the highest courage and the perfection of art, but the forces of nature as well. In spite of the advantage that an enemy, as able as he is bold, takes of these conditions, and the fact that he intrenches himself anew in his impregnable mountains, hard prest on every side, he is forced not only to allow his cannon and baggage to fall a prey to the Duc d'Enghien, but also the country bordering the Rhine. See how everything is shaken to its foundation: Philipsburg is in dire distress in ten days, in spite of the winter now close at hand; Philipsburg, which so long held the Rhine captive under our laws, and whose loss the greatest of kings so gloriously retrieved. Worms, Spire, Mayence, Landau, twenty other places I might name, open their portals: Merci is unable to defend them, and no longer faces his conqueror. It is not enough; he must fall at his feet, a worthy victim of his valor. Nordlingen will witness his overthrow; it will there be admitted that it is no more possible to withstand the French in Germany than in Flanders. And all these benefits we will owe to this self-same prince. God, the protector of France and of a king whom He has destined to perform His great works, thus ordains ...

It was not merely for a son nor for his family that he had such tender sentiments: I have seen him (and do not think that I here speak in terms of exaggeration), I have seen him deeply moved by the perils of his friends. Simple and natural as he was, I have seen his features betray his emotions at the story of their misfortunes, and he was ever ready to confer with them on the most insignificant details as well as on affairs of the utmost importance. In the adjustment of quarrels, he was ever ready to soothe turbulent spirits with a patience and good nature that one would little have expected from a disposition so excitable, nor from a character so lofty. What a contrast to heroes devoid of human sympathy! Well might the latter command respect and charm the admiration, as do all extraordinary things, but they will not win the heart. When God fashioned the heart of man and endowed him with human affection, He first of all inspired him with the quality of kindness, like unto the essence of the divine nature itself, as a token of the beneficent hand that fashioned us. Kindness, therefore, ought to be the mainspring and guide of our heart, and ought at the same time to be the chief attraction that should, as it were, be a part of our very being, with which to win the hearts of others. Greatness, which is but the result of good fortune, so far from diminishing the quality of kindness, is but given one that he might the more freely spread broadcast its beneficent effects like a public fountain, which is but erected that its waters might be scattered to the sunlight.

This is the value of a good heart; and the great who are devoid of the quality of kindness, justly punished for their disdainful insensibility to the misfortunes of their fellows, are forever deprived of the greatest blessing of human life—that is to say, of the pleasures of society. Never did man enjoy these pleasures more keenly than the prince of whom I am speaking; never was man less inspired with the misgiving that familiarity breeds contempt. Is this the man who carried cities by storm and won great battles? Verily, he seems to have forgotten the high rank he so well knew how to sustain. Do you not recognize in him the hero, who, ever equable and consistent, never having to stand on tiptoe to seem taller than he is, nor to stoop to be courteous and obliging, found himself by nature all that a man ought to be toward his fellow, like a majestic and bountiful stream, which peacefully bears into the cities the abundance it has spread in the fields that it has watered, which gives to all and never rises above its normal height, nor becomes swollen except when violent opposition is offered to the gentle slope by which it continues on its tranquil course. Such, indeed, has also been the gentleness and such the might of the Prince de Condé. Have you a secret of importance? Confide it boldly to the safe-keeping of this noble heart; he will reward your confidence by making your affair his own. To this prince nothing is more inviolable than the sacred rights of friendship. When a favor is asked of him he acts as tho he himself were under obligation; and never has a joy

79

keener and truer been witnessed than he felt at being able to give pleasure to another.

It was a grand spectacle to see during the same period, and in the same campaigns, these two men, who in the common opinion of all Europe could be favorably compared to the greatest captains of past ages, sometimes at the head of different bodies of troops; sometimes united more indeed by the concord of their thoughts than by the orders which the subaltern received from his superior; sometimes at the head of opposing forces, and each redoubling his customary activity and vigilance, as tho God, who, according to the Scriptures, often in His wisdom makes a sport of the universe, had desired to show mortals the wonders in all their forms that He could work with men. Behold the encampments, the splendid marches, the audacity, the precautions, the perils, the resources of these brave men! Has there ever been beheld in two men virtues such as these in characters so different, not to say diametrically opposite? The one appears to be guided by deep reflection, the other by sudden illumination; the latter as a consequence, tho more impetuous, yet never acting with undue precipitation; the former, colder of manner, tho never slow, is bolder of action than of speech, and even while having the outward appearance of embarrassment, inwardly determined and resolved. The one, from the moment he appears in the army, conveys an exalted idea of his worth and makes one expect of him something out of the ordinary; nevertheless, he advanced in regular order, and performed, as it were, by degrees, the prodigious deeds which marked the course of his career. The other, like a man inspired from the date of his first battle, showed himself the equal of the most consummate masters of the art of warfare. The one by his prompt and continued efforts commanded the admiration of the human race and silenced the voice of envy; the other shone so resplendently from the very beginning that none dared attack him. The one, in a word, by the depth of his genius and the incredible resources of his courage, rose superior to the greatest perils and even knew how to profit by every kind of fickleness of fortune; the other, by reason of the advantages derived from high birth, by his great conceptions derived from Heaven, and by a kind of admirable instinct, the secret of which is not given to ordinary men, seemed born to mold fortune to conform to his designs and bring destiny to his feet. And that the great tho diverse characters of these two men might be clearly discerned, it should be borne in mind that the one, his career cut short by an unexpected blow, died for his country like another Judas Maccabeus, mourned by the army as for a father, while the court and all the people, lamented his fate. His piety as well as his courage were universally lauded, and his memory will never fade from the minds of men. The other, raised to the very summit of glory by force of arms like another David, dies like him in his bed, sounding the praises of God and leaving his dying behests to his family, while all hearts were imprest as much by the splendor of his life as by the gentleness of his death.

BUNYAN

THE HEAVENLY FOOTMAN

BIOGRAPHICAL NOTE

John Bunyan was born in the village of Elstow, near Bedford, England, in 1628. Because of his fearless preaching he was imprisoned in Bedford jail from 1660 to 1672, and again for six months in 1675, during which latter time it is said his wonderful "Pilgrim's Progress" was written. While his sermons in their tedious prolixity share the fault of his time, they are characterized by vividness, epigrammatic wit, and dramatic fervor. The purity and simplicity of his style have been highly praised, and his unflinching faith has been the inspiration of many a hesitating soul. Among his best known works are "The Holy War," "Grace Abounding in the Chief of Sinners," and "Sighs from Hell." He died in London in 1688.

BUNYAN

1628-1688
THE HEAVENLY FOOTMAN

So run that ye may obtain.—I Cor. ix., 24.

Heaven and happiness is that which every one desireth, insomuch that wicked Balaam could say, "Let me die the death of the righteous, and let my last end be like his." Yet, for all this, there are but very few that do obtain that ever-to-be-desired glory, insomuch that many eminent professors drop short of a welcome from God into this pleasant place. The apostle, therefore, because he did desire the salvation of the souls of the Corinthians, to whom he writes this epistle, layeth them down in these words such counsel, which if taken, would be for their help and advantage.

First, Not to be wicked, and sit still, and wish for heaven; but to run for it.

Secondly, Not to content themselves with, every kind of running, but, saith he, "So run that ye may obtain." As if he should say, some, because they would not lose their souls, begin to run betimes, they run apace, they run with patience, they run the right way. Do you so run. Some run from both father and mother, friends and companions, and thus, they may have the crown. Do you so run. Some run through temptations, afflictions, good report, evil report, that they may win the pearl. Do you so run. "So run that ye may obtain."

These words were taken from men's funning for a wager; a very apt similitude to set before the eyes of the saints of the Lord. "Know you that they which run in a race run all, but one obtaineth the prize? So run that ye may obtain." That is, do not only run, but be sure you win as well as run. "So run that ye may obtain."

I shall not need to make any great ado in opening the words at this time, but shall rather lay down one doctrine that I do find in them; and in prosecuting that, I shall show you, in some measure, the scope of the words.

The doctrine is this: They that will have heaven, must run for it; I say, they that will have heaven, they must run for it. I beseech you to heed it well. "Know ye not, that they which run in a race run all, but one obtaineth the prize? So run ye." The prize is heaven, and if you will have it, you must run for it. You have another scripture for this in the xii. of the Hebrews, the 1st, 2d, and 3d verses: "Wherefore seeing also," saith the apostle, "that we are compassed about with so great a cloud of witnesses, let us lay aside every weight, and the sin which doth so easily beset us, and let us run with patience the race that is set before us." And let us run, saith he. Again, saith Paul, "I so run, not as uncertainly: so fight I," etc.

But before I go any farther:

1. Fleeing. Observe, that this running is not an ordinary, or any sort of running, but it is to be understood of the swiftest sort of running; and therefore, in the vi. of the Hebrews, it is called a fleeing: "That we might have strong consolation, who have fled for refuge, to lay hold on the hope set before us." Mark, who have fled. It is taken from that xx. of Joshua, concerning the man that was to flee to the city of refuge, when the avenger of blood was hard at his heels, to take vengeance on him for the offense he had committed; therefore it is a running or fleeing for one's life: a running with all might and main, as we use to say. So run.

2. Pressing. Secondly, this running in another place is called a pressing. "I press toward the mark"; which signifieth, that they that will have heaven, they must not stick at any difficulties they meet with; but press, crowd, and thrust through all that may stand between heaven and their souls. So run.

3. Continuing. Thirdly, this running is called in another place, a continuing in the way of life. "If you continue in the faith grounded, and settled, and be not moved away from the hope of the gospel of Christ." Not to run a little now and then, by fits and starts, or half-way, or almost thither, but to run for my life, to run through all difficulties, and to continue therein to the end of the race, which must be to the end of my life. "So run that ye may obtain." And the reasons are:

(1.) Because all or every one that runneth doth not obtain the prize; there may be many that do run, yea, and run far too, who yet miss of the crown that standeth at the end of the race. You know all that run in a race do not obtain the victory; they all run, but one wins. And so it is here; it is not every one that runneth, nor every one that seeketh, nor every one that striveth for the mastery that hath it. "Tho a man do strive for the mastery," saith Paul, "yet he is not crowned, unless he strive lawfully"; that is, unless he so run, and so strive, as to have God's approbation. What, do you think that every heavy-heeled professor will have heaven? What, every lazy one? every wanton and foolish professor, that will be stopt by anything, kept back by anything, that scarce runneth so fast heavenward as a snail creepeth on the ground? Nay, there are some professors that do not go on so fast in the way of God as a snail doth go on the wall; and yet these think that heaven and happiness is for them. But stay, there are many more that run than there be that obtain; therefore he that will have heaven must run for it.

(2.) Because you know, that tho a man do run, yet if he do not overcome, or win, as well as run, what will they be the better for their running? They will get nothing. You know the man that runneth, he doth do it to win the prize; but if he doth not obtain it, he doth lose his labor, spend his pains and time, and that to no purpose; I say, he getteth nothing. And ah! how many such runners will there be found in the day of judgment? Even multitudes, multitudes that have run, yea, run so far as to come to heaven-gates, and not able to get any farther, but there stand knocking when it is too late, crying, Lord! Lord! when they have nothing but rebukes for their pains. Depart from Me, you come not here, you come too late, you run too lazily; the door is shut. "When once the master of the house is risen up," saith Christ, "and hath shut to the door, and ye begin to stand without, and to knock, saying, Lord, Lord, open to us, I will say, I know you not, depart," etc. Oh, sad will the state of those be that run and miss; therefore, if you will have heaven, you must run for it; and "so run that ye may obtain."

(3.) Because the way is long (I speak metaphorically), and there is many a dirty step, many a high hill, much work to do, a wicked heart, world, and devil to overcome; I say, there are many steps to be taken by those that intend to be saved, by running or walking in the steps of that faith of our father Abraham. Out of Egypt thou must go through the Red Sea; thou must run a long and tedious journey, through the vast howling wilderness, before thou come to the land of promise.

(4.) They that will go to heaven they must run for it; because, as the way is long, so the time in which they are to get to the end of it is very uncertain; the time present is the only time; thou hast no more time allotted thee than thou now enjoyest: "Boast not thyself of to-morrow, for thou knowest not what a day may bring forth." Do not say, I have time enough to get to heaven seven years hence; for I tell thee, the bell may toll for thee before seven days more be ended; and when death comes, away thou must go, whether thou art provided or not; and therefore look to it; make no delays; it is not good dallying with things of so great concernment as the salvation or damnation of thy soul. You know he that hath a great way to go in a little time, and less by half than he thinks of, he had need to run for it.

(5.) They that will have heaven, they must run for it; because the devil, the law, sin, death, and hell follow them. There is never a poor soul that is going to heaven, but the devil, the law, sin, death, and hell, make after the soul. "The devil, your adversary, as a roaring lion, goeth about, seeking whom he may devour."

And I will assure you, the devil is nimble, he can run apace, he is light of foot, he hath overtaken many, he hath turned up their heels, and hath given them an everlasting fall. Also the law, that can shoot a great way, have a care thou keep out of the reach of those great guns, the Ten Commandments. Hell also hath a wide mouth; it can stretch itself farther that you are aware of. And as the angel said to Lot, "Take heed, look not behind thee, neither tarry thou in all the plain" (that is, anywhere between this and heaven), "lest thou be consumed"; so I say to thee, Take heed, tarry not, lest either the devil, hell or the fearful curses of the law of God do overtake thee, and throw thee down in the midst of thy sins, so as never to rise and recover again. If this were all considered, then thou, as well as I, wouldst say, They that will have heaven must run for it.

(6.) They that go to heaven must run for it; because perchance the gates of heaven may be shut shortly. Sometimes sinners have not heaven-gates open to them so long as they suppose; and if they be once shut against a man, they are so heavy that all the men in the world, nor all the angels in heaven, are not able to open them. "I shut, and no man can open," saith Christ. And how if thou shouldst come but one quarter of an hour too late? I tell thee, it will cost thee an eternity to bewail thy misery in. Francis Spira can tell thee what it is to stay till the gate of mercy be quite shut; or to run so lazily that they be shut before you get within them. What, to be shut out! what, out of heaven! Sinner, rather than lose it, run for it; yea, "and so run that thou mayst obtain."

(7.) Lastly, because if thou lose, thou losest all, thou losest soul, God, Christ, heaven, ease, peace, etc. Besides, thou layest thyself open to all the shame, contempt, and reproach, that either God, Christ, saints, the world, sin, the devil, and all can lay upon thee. As Christ saith of the foolish builder, so I will say of thee, if thou be such a one who runs and misses; I say, even all that go by will begin to mock at thee, saying, This man began to run well, but was not able to finish. But more of this anon.

Quest. But how should a poor soul do to run? For this very

thing is that which afflicteth me sore (as you say), to think that I may run, and yet fall short. Methinks to fall short at last, oh, it fears me greatly. Pray tell me, therefore, how I should run.

Ans. That thou mayst indeed be satisfied in this particular, consider these following things.

The first direction: If thou wouldst so run as to obtain the kingdom of heaven, then be sure that thou get into the way that leadeth thither: For it is a vain thing to think that ever thou shalt have the prize, tho thou runnest never so fast, unless thou art in the way that leads to it. Set the case, that there should be a man in London that was to run to York for a wager; now, tho he run never so swiftly, yet if he run full south, he might run himself quickly out of breath, and be never nearer the prize, but rather the farther off? Just so is it here; it is not simply the runner, nor yet the hasty runner, that winneth the crown, unless he be in the way that leadeth thereto. I have observed, that little time which I have been a professor, that there is a great running to and fro, some this way, and some that way, yet it is to be feared most of them are out of the way, and then, tho they run as swift as the eagle can fly, they are benefited nothing at all.

Here is one runs a-quaking, another a-ranting; one again runs after the baptism, and another after the Independency: here is one for Freewill, and another for Presbytery; and yet possibly most of all these sects run quite the wrong way, and yet every one is for his life, his soul, either for heaven or hell.

If thou now say, Which is the way? I tell thee it is Christ, the Son of Mary, the Son of God. Jesus saith, "I am the way, the truth, and the life; no man cometh to the Father but by me." So then thy business is (if thou wouldst have salvation), to see if Christ be thine, with all His benefits; whether He hath covered thee with His righteousness, whether He hath showed thee that thy sins are washed away with His heart-blood, whether thou art planted into Him, and whether you have faith in Him, so as to make a life out of Him, and to conform thee to Him; that is, such faith as to conclude that thou art righteous, because Christ is thy righteousness, and so constrained to walk with Him as the joy of thy heart, because he saveth thy soul. And for the Lord's sake take heed, and do not deceive thyself, and think thou art in the way upon too slight grounds; for if thou miss of the way, thou wilt miss of the prize, and if thou miss of that I am sure thou wilt lose thy soul, even that soul which is worth more than the whole world.

Mistrust thy own strength, and throw it away; down on thy knees in prayer to the Lord for the spirit of truth; search His word for direction; flee seducers' company; keep company with the soundest Christians, that have most experience of Christ; and be sure thou have a care of Quakers, Ranters, Free-willers: also do not have too much company with some Anabaptists, tho I go under that name myself. I will tell thee this is such a serious matter, and I fear thou wilt so little regard it, that the thought of the worth of the thing, and of thy too light regarding of it, doth even make my heart ache whilst I am writing to thee. The Lord teach thee the way by His Spirit, and then I am sure thou wilt know it. So run.

The second direction: As thou shouldst get into the way, so thou shouldst also be much in studying and musing on the way. You know men that would be expert in anything, they are usually much in studying of that thing, and so likewise is it with those that quickly grow expert in any way. This therefore thou shouldst do; let thy study be much exercised about Christ, which is the way, what He is, what He hath done, and why He is what He is, and why He hath done what is done; as why "He took upon Him the form of a servant" (Phil, ii.); why He was "made in the likeness of man"; why He cried; why He died; why He "bare the sin of the world"; why He was made sin, and why He was made righteousness; why He is in heaven in the nature of man, and what He doth there. Be much in musing and considering of these things; be thinking also enough of those places which thou must not come near, but leave some on this hand, and some on that hand; as it is with those that travel into other countries; they must leave such a gate on this hand, and such a bush on that hand, and go by such a place, where standeth such a thing. Thus therefore you must do: "Avoid such things, which are expressly forbidden in the Word of God." Withdraw thy foot far from her, "and come not nigh the door of her house, for her steps take hold of hell, going down to the chambers of death." And so of everything that is not in the way, have a care of it, that thou go not by it; come not near it, have nothing to do with it. So run.

The third direction: Not only thus, but in the next place, thou must strip thyself of those things that may hang upon thee, to the hindering of thee in the way to the kingdom of heaven, as covetousness, pride, lust, or whatever else thy heart may be inclining unto, which may hinder thee in this heavenly race. Men that run for a wager, if they intend to win as well as run, they do not use to encumber themselves, or carry those things about them that may be a hindrance to them in their running. "Every man that striveth for the mastery is temperate in all things"; that is, he layeth aside everything that would be anywise a disadvantage to him; as saith the apostle, "Let us lay aside every weight, and the sin that doth so easily beset us, and let us run with patience the race that is set before us." It is but a vain thing to talk of going to heaven, if thou let thy heart be encumbered with those things that would hinder. Would you not say that such a man would be in danger of losing, tho he run, if he fill his pockets with stones, hang heavy garments on his shoulders, and get lumpish shoes on his feet? So it is here; thou talkest of going to heaven, and yet fillest thy pockets with stones—*i.e.*, fillest thy heart with this world, lettest that hang on thy shoulders, with its profits and pleasures. Alas! alas! thou art widely mistaken: if thou intendest to win, thou must strip, thou must lay aside every weight, thou must be temperate in all things. Thou must so run.

The fourth direction: Beware of by-paths; take heed thou dost not turn into those lanes which lead out of the way. There are crooked paths, paths in which men go astray, paths that lead to death and damnation, but take heed of all those. Some of them are dangerous because of practise, some because of opinion, but mind them not; mind the path before thee, look right before thee, turn neither to the right hand nor to the left, but let thine eyes look right on, even right before thee; "Ponder the path of thy feet, and let all thy ways be established." Turn not to the right hand nor to the left. "Remove thy foot far from evil." This counsel being not so seriously taken as given, is the reason of that starting from opinion to opinion, reeling this way and that way, out of this lane into that lane, and so missing the way to the kingdom. Tho the way to heaven be but one, yet there are many crooked lanes and by-paths that shoot down upon it, as I may say. And again, notwithstanding the kingdom of heaven be the biggest city, yet usually those by-paths are most beaten, most travelers go those ways; and therefore the way to heaven is hard to be found, and as hard to be kept in, by reason of these. Yet, nevertheless, it is in this case as it was with the harlot of Jericho; she had one scarlet thread tied in her window, by which her house was known: so it is here, the scarlet streams of Christ's blood run throughout the way to the kingdom of heaven; therefore mind that, see if thou do not find the besprinkling of the blood of Christ in the way, and if thou do, be of good cheer, thou art in the right way; but have a care thou beguile not thyself with a fancy; for then thou mayst light into any lane or way; but that thou mayst not be mistaken, consider, tho it seem never so pleasant, yet if thou do not find that in the very middle of the road there is written with the heart-blood of Christ, that he came into the world to save sinners, and that we are justified, tho we are ungodly, shun that way; for this it is which the apostle meaneth when, he saith, "We have boldness to enter into the holiest by the blood of Jesus, by a new and living way which He hath consecrated for us, through the vail—that is to say, His flesh." How easy a matter it is in this our day, for the devil to be too cunning for poor souls, by calling his by-paths the way to the kingdom. If such an opinion or fancy be but cried up by one or more, this inscription being set upon it by the devil, "This is the way of God," how speedily, greedily, and by heaps, do poor simple souls throw away themselves upon it; especially if it be daubed over with a few external acts of morality, if so good. But it is because men do not know painted by-paths from the plain way to the kingdom of heaven. They have not yet learned the true Christ, and what His righteousness is, neither have they a sense of their own insufficiency; but are bold, proud, presumptuous, self-conceited. And therefore,

The fifth direction: Do not thou be too much in looking too high in thy journey heavenward. You know men that run a race do not use to stare and gaze this way and that, neither do they use to cast up their eyes too high, lest haply, through their too much gazing with their eyes after other things, they in the mean time stumble and catch a fall. The very same case is this: if thou gaze and stare after every opinion and way that comes into the world, also if thou be prying overmuch into God's secret decrees, or let thy heart too much entertain questions about some nice foolish curiosities, thou mayst stumble and fall, as many hundreds in England have done, both in ranting and quakery, to their own eternal overthrow, without the marvelous operation of God's grace be suddenly stretched forth to bring them back again. Take heed, therefore; follow not that proud, lofty spirit, that, devil-like, can not be content with his own station. David was of an excellent spirit, where he saith, "Lord, my heart is not haughty, nor mine eyes lofty, neither do I exercise myself in great matters, or things too high for me. Surely I have behaved and quieted myself as a child that is weaned of his mother: My soul is even as a weaned child." Do thou so run.

The sixth direction: Take heed that you have not an ear open to every one that calleth after you as you are in your journey. Men that run, you know, if any do call after them, saying, I would speak with you, or go not too fast and you shall have my company with you, if they run for some great matter, they use to say, Alas! I can not stay, I am in haste, pray talk not to me now; neither can I stay for you, I am running for a wager: if I win I am made; if I lose I am undone, and therefore hinder me not. Thus wise are men when they run for corruptible things, and thus shouldst thou do, and thou hast more cause to do so than they, forasmuch as they run for things that last not, but thou for an incorruptible glory. I give thee notice of this betimes, knowing that thou shalt have enough call after thee, even the devil, sin, this world, vain company, pleasures, profits, esteem among men, ease, pomp, pride, together with an innumerable company of such companions; one crying, Stay for me; the other saying, Do not leave me behind; a third saying, And take me along with you. What, will you go, saith the devil, without your sins, pleasures, and profits? Are you so hasty? Can you not stay and take these along with you? Will you leave your friends and companions behind you? Can you not do as your neighbors do, carry the world, sin, lust, pleasure, profit, esteem among men, along with you? Have a care thou do not let thine ear open to the tempting, enticing, alluring, and soul-entangling flatteries of such sink-souls as these are. "My son," saith Solomon, "if sinners entice thee, consent thou not."

You know what it cost the young man whom Solomon speaks of in the vii. of the Proverbs, that was enticed by a harlot: "With much fair speech she won him, and caused him to yield, with the flattering of her lips she forced him, till he went after her as an ox to the slaughter, or as a fool to the correction of the stocks"; even so far, "till the dart struck through his liver," and he knew not "that it was for his life." "Hearken unto me now therefore," saith he, "O ye children, and attend to the words of my mouth, let not thine heart incline to her ways, go not astray in her paths, for she hast cast down many wounded, yea, many strong men have been slain (that is, kept out of heaven); by her house is the way to hell, going down to the chambers of death." Soul, take this counsel, and say, Satan, sin, lust, pleasure, profit, pride, friends, companions, and everything else, let me alone, stand off, come not nigh me, for I am running for heaven, for my soul, for God, for Christ, from hell and everlasting damnation; if I win, I win all; and if I lose, I lose all; let me alone, for I will not hear. So run.

The seventh direction: In the next place be not daunted tho thou meetest with never so many discouragements in thy journey thither. That man that is resolved for heaven, if Satan can not win him by flatteries, he will endeavor to weaken him by discouragements; saying, Thou art a sinner, thou hath broken God's law, thou art not elected, thou cometh too late, the day of grace is passed, God doth not care for thee, thy heart is naught, thou art lazy, with a hundred other discouraging suggestions. And thus it was with David where he saith, "I had fainted, unless I had believed to see the loving-kindness of the Lord in the land of the living." As if he should say, the devil did so rage, and my heart was so base, that had I judged according to my own sense and feeling, I had been absolutely distracted; but I trusted to Christ in the promise, and looked that God would be as good as his promise, in having mercy upon me, an unworthy sinner; and this is that which encouraged me, and kept me from fainting. And thus must thou do when Satan or the law, or thy own conscience, do go about to dishearten thee, either by the greatness of thy sins, the wickedness of thy heart, the tediousness of the way, the loss of outward enjoyments, the hatred that thou wilt procure from the world or the like; then thou must encourage thyself with the freeness of the promises, the tender-heartedness of Christ, the merits of His blood, the freeness of His invitations to come in, the greatness of the sin of others that have been pardoned, and that the same God, through the same Christ, holdeth forth the same grace as free as ever. If these be not thy meditations, thou wilt draw very heavily in the way of heaven, if thou do not give up all for lost, and so knock off from following any farther; therefore, I say, take heart in thy journey, and say to them that seek thy destruction, "Rejoice not against me, O my enemy, for when I fall I shall arise, when I sit in darkness the Lord shall be a light unto me." So run.

The eighth direction: Take heed of being offended at the cross that thou must go by before thou come to heaven. You must understand (as I have already touched) that there is no man that goeth to heaven but he must go by the cross. The cross is the standing way-mark by which all they that go to glory must pass.

"We must through much tribulation enter into the kingdom of heaven." "Yea, and all that will live godly in Christ Jesus shall suffer persecution." If thou art in thy way to the kingdom, my life for thine thou wilt come at the cross shortly (the Lord grant thou dost not shrink at it, so as to turn thee back again).

"If any man will come after me," saith Christ, "let him deny himself, and take up his cross daily, and follow me." The cross it stands, and hath stood, from the beginning, as a way-mark to the kingdom of heaven. You know, if one ask you the way to such and such a place, you, for the better direction, do not only say, This is the way, but then also say, You must go by such a gate, by such a stile, such a bush, tree, bridge, or such like. Why, so it is here; art thou inquiring the way to heaven? Why, I tell thee, Christ is the way; into Him thou must get, into His righteousness, to be justified; and if thou art in Him, thou wilt presently see the cross, thou must go close by it, thou must touch it, nay, thou must take it up, or else thou wilt quickly go out of the way that leads to heaven, and turn up some of those crooked lanes that lead down to the chambers of death.

It is the cross which keepeth those that are kept from heaven. I am persuaded, were it not for the cross, where we have one professor we should have twenty; but this cross, that is it which spoileth all.

The ninth direction: Beg of God that He would do these two things for thee: First, enlighten thine understanding: And, secondly, inflame thy will. If these two be but effectually done, there is no fear but thou wilt go safe to heaven.

One of the great reasons why men and women do so little regard the other world is because they see so little of it: And the reason why they see so little of it is because they have their understanding darkened: And therefore, saith Paul, "Do not you believers walk as do other Gentiles, even in the vanity of their minds, having their understanding darkened, being alienated from the life of God through the ignorance (or foolishness) that is in them, because of the blindness of their heart." Walk not as those, run not with them: alas! poor souls, they have their understandings darkened, their hearts blinded, and that is the reason they have such undervaluing thoughts of the Lord Jesus Christ, and the salvation of their souls. For when men do come to see the things of another world, what a God, what a Christ, what a heaven, and what an eternal glory there is to be enjoyed; also when they see that it is possible for them to have a share in it, I tell you it will make them run through thick and thin to enjoy it. Moses, having a sight of this, because his understanding was enlightened, "He feared not the wrath of the king, but chose rather to suffer afflictions with the people of God than to enjoy the pleasures of sin for a season. He refused to be called the son of the king's daughter"; accounting it wonderful riches to be accounted worthy of so much as to suffer for Christ with the poor despised saints; and that was because he saw Him who was invisible, and had respect unto the recompense of reward. And this is that which the apostle usually prayeth for in his epistles for the saints, namely, "That they might know what is the hope of God's calling, and the riches of the glory of his inheritance in the saints; and that they might be able to comprehend with all saints, what is the breadth, and length, and depth, and height, and know the love of Christ, which passeth knowledge." ...

The tenth direction: Cry to God that He would inflame thy will also with the things of the other world. For when a man's will is fully set to do such or such a thing, then it must be a very hard matter that shall hinder that man from bringing about his end. When Paul's will was set resolvedly to go up to Jerusalem (tho it was signified to him before what he should there suffer), he was not daunted at all; nay, saith he, "I am ready (or willing) not only to be bound, but also to die at Jerusalem for the name of the Lord Jesus." His will was inflamed with love to Christ; and therefore all the persuasions that could be used wrought nothing at all.

Your self-willed people, nobody knows what to do with them:

we use to say, he will have his own will, do all what you can. Indeed, to have such a will for heaven, is an admirable advantage to a man that undertaketh a race thither; a man that is resolved, and hath his will fixt, saith he, I will do my best to advantage myself; I will do my worst to hinder my enemies; I will not give out as long as I can stand; I will have it or I will lose my life; "tho he slay me, yet will I trust in him. I will not let thee go except thou bless me." I will, I will, I will, oh this blest inflamed will for heaven! What is it like? If a man be willing, then any argument shall be a matter of encouragement; but if unwilling, then any argument shall give discouragement; this is seen both in saints and sinners; in them that are the children of God, and also those that are the children of the devil. As,

1. The saints of old, they being willing and resolved for heaven, what could stop them? Could fire and fagot, sword or halter, stinking dungeons, whips, bears, bulls, lions, cruel rackings, stoning, starving, nakedness, etc., "and in all these things they were more than conquerors, through him that loved them"; who had also made them "willing in the day of his power."

2. See again, on the other side, the children of the devil, because they are not willing, how many shifts and starting-holes they will have. I have a married wife, I have a farm, I shall offend my landlord, I shall offend my master, I shall lose my trading, I shall lose my pride, my pleasures, I shall be mocked and scoffed, therefore I dare not come. I, saith another, will stay till I am older, till my children are out, till I am got a little aforehand in the world, till I have done this and that and the other business; but, alas! the thing is, they are not willing; for, were they but soundly willing, these, and a thousand such as these, would hold them no faster than the cords held Samson, when he broke them like burnt flax. I tell you the will is all: that is one of the chief things which turns the wheel either backward or forward; and God knoweth that full well, and so likewise doth the devil; and therefore they both endeavor very much to strengthen the will of their servants; God, He is for making of His a willing people

to serve Him; and the devil, he doth what he can to possess the will and affection of those that are his with love to sin; and therefore when Christ comes closer to the matter, indeed, saith He, "You will not come to me. How often would I have gathered you as a hen doth her chickens, but you would not." The devil had possest their wills, and so long he was sure enough of them. Oh, therefore cry hard to God to inflame thy will for heaven and Christ: thy will, I say, if that be rightly set for heaven, thou wilt not be beat off with discouragements; and this was the reason that when Jacob wrestled with the angel, tho he lost a limb, as it were, and the hollow of his thigh was put out of joint as he wrestled with him, yet saith he, "I will not," mark, "I will not let thee go except thou bless me." Get thy will tipped with the heavenly grace, and resolution against all discouragements, and then thou goest full speed for heaven; but if thou falter in thy will, and be not found there, thou wilt run hobbling and halting all the way thou runnest, and also to be sure thou wilt fall short at last. The Lord give thee a will and courage.

Thus I have done with directing thee how to run to the kingdom; be sure thou keep in memory what I have said unto thee, lest thou lose thy way. But because I would have thee think of them, take all in short in this little bit of paper.

1. Get into the way. 2. Then study on it. 3. Then, strip, and lay aside everything that would hinder. 4.. Beware of by-paths. 5. Do not gaze and stare too much about thee, but be sure to ponder the path of thy feet. 6. Do not stop for any that call after thee, whether it be the world, the flesh, or the devil: for all these will hinder thy journey, if possible. 7. Be not daunted with any discouragements thou meetest with as thou goest. 8. Take heed of stumbling at the cross. 9. Cry hard to God for an enlightened heart, and a willing mind, and God give thee a prosperous journey.

Provocation: Now that you may be provoked to run with the foremost, take notice of this. When Lot and his wife were running from curst Sodom to the mountains, to save their lives, it is said, that his wife looked back from behind him, and she became a pillar of salt; and yet you see that neither her example, nor the judgment of God that fell upon her for the same, would cause Lot to look behind him. I have sometimes wondered at Lot in this particular; his wife looked behind her, and died immediately, but let what would become of her, Lot would not so much as once look behind him to see her. We do not read that he did so much as once look where she was, or what was become of her; his heart was indeed upon his journey, and well it might: there was the mountain before him, and the fire and brimstone behind him; his life lay at stake, and he had lost it if he had looked behind. Do thou so run and in thy race remember Lot's wife, and remember her doom; and remember for what that doom did overtake her; and remember that God made her an example for all lazy runners, to the end of the world; and take heed thou fall not after the same example. But,

If this will not provoke thee, consider thus, 1. Thy soul is thine own soul, that is either to be saved or lost; thou shalt not lose my soul by thy laziness. It is thine own soul, thine own ease, thine own peace, thine own advantage or disadvantage. If it were my own that thou art desired to be good unto, methinks reason should move thee somewhat to pity it. But, alas! it is thine own, thine own soul. "What shall it profit a man if he shall gain the whole world, and lose his own soul?" God's people wish well to the souls of others, and wilt not thou wish well to thine own? And if this will not provoke thee, then think.

Again, 2. If thou lose thy soul, it is thou also that must bear the blame. It made Cain stark mad to consider that he had not looked to his brother Abel's soul. How much more will it perplex thee to think that thou hadst not a care of thine own? And if this will not provoke thee to bestir thyself, think again.

3. That, if thou wilt not run, the people of God are resolved to deal with thee even as Lot dealt with his wife—that is, leave thee behind them. It may be thou hast a father, mother, brother, etc., going post-haste to heaven, wouldst thou be willing to be left behind them? Surely no.

Again, 4. Will it not be a dishonor to thee to see the very boys and girls in the country to have more with them than thyself? It may be the servants of some men, as the housekeeper, plowman, scullion, etc., are more looking after heaven than their masters. I am apt to think, sometimes, that more servants than masters, that more tenants than landlords, will inherit the kingdom of heaven. But is not this a shame for them that are such? I am persuaded you scorn that your servants should say that they are wiser than you in the things of this world; and yet I am bold to say that many of them are wiser than you in the things of the world to come, which are of greater concernment.

Expostulation. Well, then, sinner, what sayest thou? Where is thy heart? Wilt thou run? Art thou resolved to strip? Or art thou not? Think quickly, man; have no dallying in this matter. Confer not with flesh and blood; look up to heaven, and see how thou likest it; also to hell, and accordingly devote thyself. If thou dost not know the way, inquire at the Word of God; if thou wantest company, cry for God's Spirit; if thou wantest encouragement, entertain the promises. But be sure thou begin betimes; get into the way, run apace, and hold out to the end; and the Lord give thee a prosperous journey. Farewell.

TILLOTSON

THE REASONABLENESS OF A RESURRECTION

BIOGRAPHICAL NOTE

John Tillotson, archbishop of Canterbury, renowned as a preacher, was born at Sowerby, in Yorkshire, in 1630, the son of an ardent Independent. After graduating from Clare College, Cambridge, he began to preach in 1661, in connection with the Presbyterian wing of the Church of England. He, however, submitted to the Act of Uniformity the following year, and in 1663 was inducted into the rectory of Veddington, Suffolk. He was also appointed preacher to Lincoln's Inn, was made prebendary of Canterbury in 1670 and dean in 1672. William III regarded him with high favor, and he succeeded the nonjuring Sancroft in the arch-see of Canterbury. His sermons are characterized by stateliness, copiousness and lucidity, and were long looked upon as models of correct pulpit style. He died in 1694.

TILLOTSON

1630-1694

THE REASONABLENESS OF A RESURRECTION

Why should it be thought a thing incredible with you that God should raise the dead?—Acts xxvi., 8.

The resurrection of the dead is one of the great articles of the Christian faith; and yet so it hath happened that this great article of our religion hath been made one of the chief objections against it. There is nothing that Christianity hath been more upbraided for withal, both by the heathens of old and by the infidels of later times, than the impossibility of this article; so that it is a matter of great consideration and consequence to vindicate our religion in this particular. But if the thing be evidently impossible, then it is highly unreasonable to propose it to the belief of mankind.

I know that some, more devout than wise, and who, it is to be hoped, mean better than they understand, make nothing of impossibilities in matters of faith, and would fain persuade us that the more impossible anything is, for that very reason it is the fitter to be believed; and that it is an argument of a poor and low faith to believe only things that are possible; but a generous and heroical faith will swallow contradictions with as much ease as reason assents to the plainest and most evident propositions. Tertullian, in the heat of his zeal and eloquence, upon this point of the death and resurrection of Christ, lets fall a very odd passage, and which must have many grains of allowance to make it tolerable: "*prosus credible est* (saith he), *quia ineptum est; certum est, quia impossible*—it is therefore very credible, because it is foolish, and certain, because it is impossible";

"and this (says he) is *necessarium dedecus fidei*," that is, "it is necessary the Christian faith should be thus disgraced by the belief of impossibilities and contradictions." I suppose he means that this article of the resurrection was not in itself the less credible because the heathen philosophers caviled at it as a thing impossible and contradictious, and endeavored to disgrace the Christian religion upon that account. For if he meant otherwise, that the thing was therefore credible because it was really and in itself foolish and impossible; this had been to recommend the Christian religion from the absurdity of the things to be believed; which would be a strange recommendation of any religion to the sober and reasonable part of mankind.

I know not what some men may find in themselves; but I must freely acknowledge that I could never yet attain to that bold and hardy degree of faith as to believe anything for this reason, because it was impossible: for this would be to believe a thing to be because I am sure it can not be. So that I am very far from being of his mind, that wanted not only more difficulties, but even impossibilities in the Christian religion, to exercise his faith upon.

Leaving to the Church of Rome that foolhardiness of faith, to believe things to be true which at the same time their reason plainly tells them are impossible, I shall at this time endeavor to assert and vindicate this article of the resurrection from the pretended impossibility of it. And I hope, by God's assistance, to make the possibility of the thing so plain as to leave no considerable scruple about it in any free and unprejudiced mind. And this I shall do from these words of St. Paul, which are part of the defense which he made for himself before Festus and Agrippa, the substance whereof is this, that he had lived a blameless and inoffensive life among the Jews, in whose religion he had been bred up; that he was of the strictest sect of that religion, a Pharisee, which, in opposition to the Sadducees, maintained the resurrection of the dead and a future state of rewards and punishments in another life; and that for the hope of this he was called in question, and accused by the Jews. "And now I stand here, and am judged, for the hope of the promise made unto the fathers; unto which promise our twelve scribes, instantly serving God day and night, hope to come; for which hope's sake, King Agrippa, I am accused of the Jews." That is, he was accused for preaching that Jesus was risen from the dead, which is a particular instance of the general doctrine of the resurrection which was entertained by the greatest part of the Jews, and which to the natural reason of mankind (however the heathen in opposition to the Christian religion were prejudiced against it), hath nothing in it that is incredible. And for this he appeals to his judges, Festus and Agrippa: "why should it be thought a thing incredible with you that God should raise the dead?"

Which words being a question without an answer, imply in them these two propositions:

First, That it was thought by some a thing incredible that the dead should be raised. This is supposed in the question, as the foundation of it: for he who asks why a thing is so, supposeth it to be so.

Secondly, That this apprehension, that it is a thing incredible that God should raise the dead, is very unreasonable. For the question being left unanswered, implies its own answer, and is to be resolved into this affirmative, that there is no reason why they or any man else should think it a thing incredible that God should raise the dead.

I shall speak to these two propositions as briefly as I can; and then show what influence this doctrine of the resurrection ought to have upon our lives.

First, that it was thought by some a thing incredible that God should raise the dead. This St. Paul has reason to suppose, having from his own experience found men so averse from the entertaining of this doctrine. When he preached to the philosophers at Athens, and declared to them the resurrection of one Jesus from the dead, they were amazed at this new doctrine, and knew not what he meant by it. They said, "he seemeth to be a setter forth of strange gods, because he preached unto them Jesus and the resurrection." He had discoursed to them of the resurrection of one Jesus from the dead; but this business of the resurrection of one Jesus from the dead was a thing so remote from their apprehensions that they had no manner of conception of it; but understood him quite in another sense, as if he had declared to them two new deities, Jesus and Anastasis; as if he had brought a new god and a new goddess among them, Jesus and the Resurrection. And when he discoursed to them again more fully of this matter, it is said that, "when they heard of the resurrection of the dead, they mocked." And at the twenty-fourth verse of this twenty-sixth chapter, when he spake of the resurrection, Festus told him he would hear him no further, and that he looked upon him as a man beside himself, whom much learning had made mad. Festus looked upon this business of the resurrection as the wild speculation of a crazy head. And indeed the heathens generally, even those who believed the immortality of the soul, and another state after this life, looked upon the resurrection of the body as a thing impossible. Pliny, I remember, reckons it among those things which are impossible, and which God himself can not do; "*revocare defunctos*, to call back the dead to life"; and in the primitive times the heathen philosophers very much derided the Christians, upon account of this strange doctrine of the resurrection, looking always upon this article of their faith as a ridiculous and impossible assertion.

So easy it is for prejudice to blind the minds of men, and to represent everything to them which hath a great appearance of difficulty in it as impossible. But I shall endeavor to show that if the matter be thoroughly examined, there is no ground for any such apprehension.

I proceed therefore to the second proposition, namely, that this apprehension, that it is an incredible thing that God should raise the dead, is very unreasonable: "why should it be thought a thing incredible with you, that God should raise the dead?" That is, there is no sufficient reason why any man should look upon the resurrection of the dead as a thing impossible to the power of God; the only reason why they thought it incredible being because they judged it impossible; so that nothing can be vainer than for men to pretend to believe the resurrection; and yet at the same time to grant it to be a thing in reason impossible, because no man can believe that which he thinks to be incredible; and the impossibility of a thing is the best reason any man can have to think a thing incredible. So that the meaning of St. Paul's question is, "why should it be thought a thing impossible that God should raise the dead?"

To come then to the business: I shall endeavor to show that there is no sufficient reason why men should look upon the resurrection of the dead as a thing impossible to God. "Why should it be thought a thing incredible (that is, impossible) with you, that God should raise the dead?" which question implies in it these three things:

1. That it is above the power of nature to raise the dead.

2. But it is not above the power of God to raise the dead.

3. That God should be able to do this is by no means incredible to natural reason.

First. This question implies that it is above the power of nature to raise the dead; and therefore the apostle puts the question very cautiously, "why should it be thought incredible that God should raise the dead?" by which he seems to grant that it is impossible to any natural power to raise the dead; which is granted on all hands.

Secondly. But this question does plainly imply that it is not above the power of God to do this. Tho the raising of the dead to life be a thing above the power of nature, yet why should it be thought incredible that God, who is the author of nature, should be able to do this? and indeed the apostle's putting the question in this manner takes away the main ground of the objection against the resurrection from the impossibility of the thing. For the main reason why it was looked upon as impossible was, because it was contrary to the course of nature that there should be any return from a perfect privation to a habit, and that a body perfectly dead should be restored to life again: but for all this no man that believes in a God who made the world, and this natural frame of things, but must think it very reasonable to believe that He can do things far above the power of anything that He hath made.

Thirdly. This question implies that it is not a thing incredible to natural reason that God should be able to raise the dead. I do not say that by natural light we can discover that God will raise the dead; for that, depending merely upon the will of God, can no otherwise be certainly known than by divine revelation: but that God can do this is not at all incredible to natural reason. And this is sufficiently implied in the question which St. Paul asks, in which he appeals to Festus and Agrippa, neither of them Christians, "why should it be thought a thing incredible with you that God should raise the dead?" And why should he appeal to them concerning the credibility of this matter if it be a thing incredible to natural reason?

That it is not, I shall first endeavor to prove, and then to answer the chief objections against the possibility of it.

And I prove it thus: it is not incredible to natural reason that God made the world, and all the creatures in it; that mankind is His offspring; and that He gives us life and breath, and all things. This was acknowledged and firmly believed by many of the heathens. And indeed, whoever believes that the being of God may be known by natural light, must grant that it may be known by the natural light of reason that God made the world; because one of the chief arguments of the being of God is taken from those visible effects of wisdom, and power, and goodness, which we see in the frame of the world. Now He that can do the greater can undoubtedly do the less; He that made all things of nothing, can much more raise a body out of dust; He who at first gave life to so many inanimate beings, can easily restore that which is dead to life again. It is an excellent saying of one of the Jewish rabbis: He who made that which was not, to be, can certainly make that which was once, to be again. This hath the force of a demonstration; for no man that believes that God hath done the one, can make any doubt but that He can, if He please, do the other.

This seems to be so very clear, that they must be strong objections indeed, that can render it incredible.

There are but two that I know of, that are of any consideration, and I shall not be afraid to represent them to you with their utmost advantage; and they are these:

First, against the resurrection in general: it is pretended impossible, after the bodies of men are resolved into dust, to re-collect all the dispersed parts and bring them together, to be united into one body.

The second is leveled against a resurrection in some particular instances, and pretends it to be impossible in some cases only— viz., when that which was the matter of one man's body does afterward become the matter of another man's body; in which case, say they, it is impossible that both these should, at the resurrection, each have his own body.

The difficulty of both these objections is perfectly avoided by those who hold that it is not necessary that our bodies at the resurrection should consist of the very same parts of matter that they did before. There being no such great difference between one parcel of dust and another; neither in respect of the power of God, which can easily command this parcel of dust as that to become a living body and being united to a living soul to rise up and walk; so that the miracle of the resurrection will be all one in the main, whether our bodies be made of the very same matter they were before, or not; nor will there be any difference as to us; for whatever matter our bodies be made of, when they are once reunited to our souls, they will be then as much our own as if they had been made of the very same matter of which they consisted before. Besides that, the change which the resurrection will make in our bodies will be so great that we could not know them to be the same, tho they were so.

Now upon this supposition, which seems philosophical enough, the force of both these objections is wholly declined. But there is no need to fly to this refuge; and therefore I will take this article of the resurrection in the strictest sense for the raising of a body to life, consisting of the same individual matter that it did before; and in this sense, I think, it has generally been received by Christians, not without ground, from Scripture. I will only mention one text, which seems very strongly to imply it: "and the sea gave up the dead which were in it; and death and the grave delivered up the dead which, were in them; and they were judged every man according to his works." Now why should the sea and the grave be said to deliver up their dead, if there were not a resurrection of the same body; for any dust formed into a living body and united to the soul, would serve the turn? We will therefore take it for granted that the very same body will be raised, and I doubt not, even in this sense, to vindicate the possibility of the resurrection from both these objections.

First, against the resurrection in general of the same body; it is pretended impossible, after the bodies of men are moldered into dust, and by infinite accidents have been scattered up and down the world, and have undergone a thousand changes, to re-collect and rally together the very same parts of which they consisted before. This the heathens used to object to the primitive Christians; for which reason they also used to burn the bodies of the martyrs, and to scatter their ashes in the air, to be blown about by the wind, in derision of their hopes of a resurrection.

I know not how strong malice might make this objection to appear; but surely in reason it is very weak; for it wholly depends upon a gross mistake of the nature of God and his providence, as if it did not extend to the smallest things; as if God did not know all things that He hath made, and had them not always in His view, and perfectly under His command; and as if it were a trouble and burden to infinite knowledge and power to understand and order the least things; whereas infinite knowledge and power can know and manage all things with as much ease as we can understand

and order any one thing; so that this objection is grounded upon a low and false apprehension of the Divine nature, and is only fit for Epicurus and his herd, who fancied to themselves a sort of slothful and unthinking deities, whose happiness consisted in their laziness, and a privilege to do nothing.

I proceed therefore to the second objection, which is more close and pressing; and this is leveled against the resurrection in some particular instances. I will mention but two, by which all the rest may be measured and answered.

One is, of those who are drowned in the sea, and their bodies eaten up by fishes, and turned into their nourishment: and those fishes perhaps eaten afterward by men, and converted into the substance of their bodies.

The other is of the cannibals; some of whom, as credible relations tell us, have lived wholly or chiefly on the flesh of men; and consequently the whole, or the greater part of the substance of their bodies is made of the bodies of other men. In these and the like cases, wherein one man's body is supposed to be turned into the substance of another man's body, how should both these at the resurrection each recover his own body? So that this objection is like that of the Sadducees to our Savior, concerning a woman that had seven husbands: they ask, "whose wife of the seven shall she be at the resurrection?" So here, when several have had the same body, whose shall it be at the resurrection? and how shall they be supplied that have it not?

This is the objection; and in order to the answering of it, I shall premise these two things:

1. That the body of man is not a constant and permanent thing, always continuing in the same state, and consisting of the same matter; but a successive thing, which is continually spending and continually renewing itself, every day losing something of the matter which it had before, and gaining new; so that most men have new bodies oftener than they have new clothes; only with this difference, that we change our clothes commonly at once, but our bodies by degrees.

And this is undeniably certain from experience. For so much as our bodies grow, so much new matter is added to them, over and beside the repairing of what is continually spent; and after a man come to his full growth, so much of his food as every day turns into nourishment, so much of his yesterday's body is usually wasted, and carried off by insensible perspiration—that is, breathed out at the pores of his body; which, according to the static experiment of Sanctorius, a learned physician, who, for several years together, weighed himself exactly every day, is (as I remember) according to the proportion of five to eight of all that a man eats and drinks. Now, according to this proportion, every man must change his body several times in a year.

It is true indeed the more solid parts of the body, as the bones, do not change so often as the fluid and fleshy; but that they also do change is certain, because they grow, and whatever grows is nourished and spends, because otherwise it would not need to be repaired.

2. The body which a man hath at any time of his life is as much his own body as that which he hath at his death; so that if the very matter of his body which a man had at any time of his life be raised, it is as much his own and the same body as that which he had at his death, and commonly much more perfect; because they who die of lingering sickness or old age are usually mere skeletons when they die; so that there is no reason to suppose that the very matter of which our bodies consists at the time of our death shall be that which shall be raised, that being commonly the worst and most imperfect body of all the rest.

These two things being premised, the answer to this objection can not be difficult. For as to the more solid and firm parts of the body, as the skull and bones, it is not, I think, pretended that the cannibals eat them; and if they did, so much of the matter even of these solid parts wastes away in a few years, as being collected together would supply them many times over. And as for the fleshy and fluid parts, these are so very often changed and renewed that we can allow the cannibals to eat them all up, and to turn them all into nourishment, and yet no man need contend for want of a body of his own at the resurrection—viz., any of those bodies which he had ten or twenty years before; which are every whit as good and as much his own as that which was eaten.

Having thus shown that the resurrection is not a thing incredible to natural reason, I should now proceed to show the certainty of it from divine revelation. For as reason tells us it is not impossible, so the word of God hath assured us that it is certain. The texts of Scripture are so many and clear to this purpose, and so well known to all Christians, that I will produce none. I shall only tell you that as it is expressly revealed in the gospel, so our blest Savior, for the confirmation of our faith and the comfort and encouragement of our hope, hath given us the experiment of it in his own resurrection, which is "the earnest and first-fruits of ours." So St. Paul tells us that "Christ is risen from the dead, and become the first-fruits of them that slept" And that Christ did really rise from the dead, we have as good evidence as for any ancient matter of fact which we do most firmly believe; and more and greater evidence than this the thing is not capable of; and because it is not, no reasonable man ought to require it.

Now what remains but to conclude this discourse with those practical inferences which our apostle makes from this doctrine of the resurrection; and I shall mention these two:

The first for our support and comfort under the infirmities and miseries of this mortal life.

The second for the encouragement of obedience and a good life.

1. For our comfort and support under the infirmities and miseries of this mortal state. The consideration of the glorious change of our bodies at the resurrection of the just can not but be a great comfort to us, under all bodily pain and sufferings.

One of the greatest burdens of human nature is the frailty and infirmity of our bodies, the necessities they are frequently prest withal, the manifold diseases they are liable to, and the dangers and terrors of death, to which they are continually subject and enslaved. But the time is coming, if we be careful to prepare ourselves for it, when we shall be clothed with other kind of bodies, free from all the miseries and inconveniences which flesh and blood is subject to. For "these vile bodies shall be changed, and fashioned like to the glorious body of the Son of God." When our bodies shall be raised to a new life, they shall become incorruptible; "for this corruptible shall put on incorruption, and this mortal must put on immortality; and then shall be brought to pass the saying that is written, death is swallowed up in victory." When this last enemy is conquered, there shall be no "fleshly lusts" nor brutish passions "to fight against the soul; no law in our members to war against the laws of our minds"; no disease to torment us; no danger of death to amaze and terrify us. Then all the passions and appetites of our outward man shall be subject to the reason of our minds, and our bodies shall partake of the immortality of our souls. It is but a very little while that our spirits shall be crusht and clogged with these heavy and sluggish bodies; at the resurrection they shall be refined from all dregs of corruption, and become spiritual, and incorruptible, and glorious, and every way suited to the activity and perfection of a glorified soul and the "spirits of just men made perfect."

2. For the encouragement of obedience and a good life. Let the belief of this great article of our faith have the same influence upon us which St. Paul tells it had upon him. "I have hope toward God that there shall be a resurrection of the dead, both of the just and unjust; and herein do I exercise myself always to have a conscience void of offense toward God and toward man." The firm belief of a resurrection to another life should make every one of us very careful how we demean ourselves in this life, and afraid to do anything or to neglect anything that may defeat our hopes of a blest immortality, and expose us to the extreme and endless misery of body and soul in another life.

Particularly, it should be an argument to us, "to glorify God in our bodies and in our spirits"; and to use the members of the one and the faculties of the other as "instruments of righteousness unto holiness." We should reverence ourselves, and take heed not only how we defile our souls by sinful passions, but how we dishonor our bodies by sensual and brutish lusts; since God hath designed so great an honor and happiness for both at the resurrection.

So often as we think of a blest resurrection to eternal life, and the happy consequences of it, the thought of so glorious a reward should make us diligent and unwearied in the service of so good a Master and so great a Prince, who can and will prefer us to infinitely greater honors than any that are to be had in this world. This inference the apostle makes from the doctrine of the resurrection. "Therefore, my beloved brethren, be ye steadfast, immovable, always abounding in the work of the Lord; for as much as ye know that your labor is not in vain in the Lord."

Nay, we may begin this blest state while we are upon earth, by "setting our hearts and affections upon the things that are above, and having our conversation in heaven, from whence also we look for a Savior, the Lord Jesus Christ, who shall change our vile bodies, that they may be fashioned like unto his glorious body, according to the working whereby he is able to subdue all things to himself."

"Now the God of peace, who brought again from the dead our Lord Jesus Christ, the great Shepherd of the sheep, through the blood of the everlasting covenant, make us perfect in every good work to do his will, working in us always that which is pleasing in his sight, through Jesus Christ, to whom be glory forever. Amen."

HOWE

THE REDEEMER'S TEARS OVER LOST SOULS

BIOGRAPHICAL NOTE

John Howe, a leading writer and divine under the Commonwealth, was born in 1630, at Loughborough, in Leicestershire, England. He was educated at Cambridge and Oxford, and ordained by Charles Herle, rector of Winwick, whom he styled, "a primitive bishop." He became chaplain to Cromwell and his son Richard. Among his contributions to Puritan theology are "The Good Man the Living Temple of God," and "Vanity of Men as Mortal," He was a man of intellect and imagination. His sermons, tho often long and cumbersome, are marked by warmth of fancy and a sublimity of spirit superior to his style. Howe was a leading spirit in the effort made for the union of the Congregational and Presbyterian bodies. He died in 1705.

HOWE

1630-1705

THE REDEEMER'S TEARS OVER LOST SOULS

And when He was come near, He beheld the city, and wept over it, saying, If thou hadst known, even thou, at least in this thy day, the things which belong to thy peace! But now they are hid from thine eyes.—Luke six., 41, 42.

Such as live tinder the gospel have a day, or a present opportunity, for the obtaining the knowledge of those things immediately belonging to their peace, and of whatsoever is besides necessary thereunto. I say nothing what opportunities they have who never lived under the gospel, who yet no doubt might generally know more than they do, and know better what they do know. It suffices who enjoy the gospel to understand our own advantages thereby. Nor, as to those who do enjoy it, is every one's day of equal clearness. How few, in comparison, have ever seen such a day as Jerusalem at this time did I made by the immediate beams of the Sun of Righteousness! our Lord Himself vouchsafing to be their Instructor, so speaking as never man did, and with such authority as far outdid their other teachers, and astonished the hearers. In what transports did He use to leave those that heard Him, wheresoever He came, wondering at the gracious words that came out of His mouth! And with what mighty and beneficial works was He went to recommend His doctrine, shining in the glorious power and savoring of the abundant mercy of Heaven, so that every apprehensive mind might see the Deity was incarnate. God was come down to entreat with men, and allure them into the knowledge and love

121

of Himself. The Word was made flesh. What unprejudiced mind might not perceive it to be so? He was there manifested and vailed at once; both expressions are made concerning the same matter. The divine beams were somewhat obscured, but did yet ray through that vail; so that His glory was beheld of the only-begotten Son of His Father, full of grace and truth.

This Sun shone with a mild and benign, but with a powerful, vivifying light. In Him was life, and that life was the light of men. Such a light created unto the Jews this their day. Happy Jews, if they had understood their own happiness! And the days that followed to them (for a while) and the Gentile world were not inferior, in some respects brighter and more glorious (the more copious gift of the Holy Ghost being reserved unto the crowning and enthroning of the victorious Redeemer), when the everlasting gospel flew like lightning to the uttermost ends of the earth, and the word which began to be spoken by the Lord Himself was confirmed by them that heard Him, God also Himself bearing them witness with signs, and wonders, and gifts of the Holy Ghost. No such day hath been seen this many an age. Yet whithersoever this same gospel, for substance, comes, it also makes a day of the same kind, and affords always true tho diminished light, whereby, however, the things of our peace might be understood and known. The written gospel varies not, and if it be but simply and plainly proposed tho to some it be proposed with more advantage, to some with less, still we have the same things immediately relating to our peace extant before our eyes ...

This day hath its bounds and limits, so that when it is over and lost with such, the things of their peace are forever hid from their eyes. And that this day is not infinite and endless, we see in the present instance. Jerusalem had her day; but that day had its period, we see it comes to this at last, that now the things of her peace are hid from her eyes. We generally see the same thing, in that sinners are so earnestly prest to make use of the present time. To-day if you will hear His voice, harden not your hearts.

They are admonished to seek the Lord while He may be found, to call upon Him when He is nigh. It seems some time He will not be found, and will be far off. They are told this is the accepted time, this is the day of salvation ... As it is certain death ends the day of grace with every unconverted person, soit is very possible that it may end with divers before they die; by their total loss of all external means, or by the departure of the blest Spirit of God from them; so as to return and visit them no more.

How the day of grace may end with a person, is to be understood by considering what it is that makes up and constitutes such a day. There must become measure and proportion of time to make up this (or any) day, which is as the substratum and ground fore-laid. Then there must be light superadded, otherwise it differs not from night, which may have the same measure of mere time. The gospel revelation some way or other, must be had, as being the light of such a day. And again there must be some degree of liveliness, and vital influence, the more usual concomitant of light; the night doth more dispose men to drowsiness. The same sun that enlightens the world disseminates also an invigorating influence. If the Spirit of the living God do no way animate the gospel revelation, and breathe in it, we have no day of grace. It is not only a day of light, but a day of power, wherein souls can be wrought upon, and a people made willing to become the Lord's. As the Redeemer revealed in the gospel, is the light of the world, so He is life to it too, tho neither are planted or do take root everywhere. In Him was life and that life was the light of men. That light that rays from Him is vital light in itself, and in its tendency and design, tho it be disliked and not entertained by the most. Whereas therefore these things must concur to make up such a day; if either a man's time, his life on earth, expire, or if light quite fail him, or if all gracious influence be withheld, so as to be communicated no more, his day is done, the season of grace is over with him. Now it is plain that many a one may lose the gospel before his life end; and possible that all gracious influence may be restrained, while as yet the external dispensation of the gospel remains. A sinner may have hardened his heart to that degree that God will attempt him no more, in any kind, with any design of kindness to him, not in that more inward, immediate way at all—*i.e.*, by the motions of His Spirit, which peculiarly can impart nothing but friendly inclination, as whereby men are personally applied unto, so that can not be meant; nor by the voice of the gospel, which may either be continued for the sake of others, or they contained under it, but for their heavier doom at length. Which, tho it may seem severe, is not to be thought strange, much less unrighteous.

It is not to be thought strange to them that read the Bible, which so often speaks this sense; as when it warns and threatens men with so much terror. For if we sin wilfully after that we have received the knowledge of the truth, there remaineth no more sacrifice for sins, but a fearful looking for judgment, and fiery indignation, which shall devour the adversaries. He that despised Moses's law died without mercy, under two or three witnesses; of how much sorer punishment, suppose ye, shall he be thought worthy who hath trodden under foot the Son of God, and hath counted the blood of the covenant, wherewith He was sanctified, an unholy thing, and hath done despite unto the Spirit of grace? And when It tells us, after many overtures made to men in vain, of His having given them up. "But my people would not hearken to my voice; and Israel would none of me; so I gave them up unto their own hearts' lust: and they walked in their own counsels;" and pronounces, "Let him that is unjust be unjust still, and let him which is filthy be filthy still," and says, "In thy filthiness is lewdness, because I have purged thee, and thou wast not purged; thou shalt not be purged from thy filthiness any more, till I have caused my fury to rest upon thee." Which passages seem to imply a total desertion of them, and retraction of all gracious influence. And when it speaks of letting them be under the gospel, and the ordinary means of salvation, for the most direful purpose: as that, "This child (Jesus) was set for the fall, as well as for the rising, of many in

Israel"; as that, "Behold, I lay in Zion a stumbling, and a rock of offense"; and, "The stone which the builders refused, is made a stone of stumbling, and a rock of offense, even to them which, stumble at the word, being disobedient, whereunto also they were appointed"; with that of our Savior Himself, "For judgment I am come into this world, that they which see not might see; and that they which see, might be made blind." And most agreeable to those former places is that of the prophet, "But the word of the Lord was unto them precept upon precept, line upon line, here a little and there a little; that they might go, and fall backward, and be broken, and snared, and taken." And we may add, that our God hath put us out of doubt that there is such a sin as that which is eminently called the sin against the Holy Ghost; that a man in such circumstances, and to such a degree, sin against that Spirit, that He will never move or breathe upon him more, but leave him to a hopeless ruin; tho I shall not in this discourse determine or discuss the nature of it. But I doubt not it is somewhat else than final impenitency and infidelity; and that every one that dies, not having sincerely repented and believed, is not guilty of it, tho every one that is guilty of it dies impenitent and unbelieving, but was guilty of it before; so it is not the mere want of time that makes him guilty. Whereupon, therefore, that such may outlive their day of grace, is out of the question ...

Wherefore, no man can certainly know, or ought to conclude, concerning himself or others, as long as they live, that the season of grace is quite over with them. As we can conceive no rule God hath set to Himself to proceed by, in ordinary cases of this nature; so nor is there any He hath set unto us to judge by, in this case. It were to no purpose, and could be of no use to men to know so much; therefore it were unreasonable to expect God should have settled and declared any rule, by which they might come to the knowledge of it. As the case is then, viz.: there being no such rule, no such thing can be concluded; for who can tell what an arbitrary, sovereign, free agent will do, if he declare not his own purpose himself? How should it be known, when the Spirit of God hath been often working upon the soul of man, that this or that shall be the last act, and that he will never put forth another? And why should God make it known? To the person himself whose case it is, 'tis manifest it could be of no benefit. Nor is it to be thought the Holy God will ever so alter the course of His own proceedings but that it shall be finally seen to all the world that every man's destruction was entirely, and to the last, of himself. If God had made it evident to a man that he were finally rejected, he were obliged to believe it. But shall it ever be said, God hath made anything a man's duty which were inconsistent with his felicity. The having sinned himself into such a condition wherein he is forsaken of God is indeed inconsistent with it. And so the case is to stand—*i.e.*, that his perdition be in immediate connection with his sin, not with his duty; as it would be in immediate, necessary connection with his duty, if he were bound to believe himself finally forsaken and a lost creature. For that belief makes him hopeless, and a very devil, justifies his unbelief in the gospel, toward himself, by removing and shutting up, toward himself, the object of such a faith, and consequently brings the matter to this state that he perishes, not because he doth not believe God reconcilable to man, but because, with particular application to himself, he ought not so to believe. And it were most unfit, and of very pernicious consequence, that such a thing should be generally known concerning others....

But tho none ought to conclude that their day or season of grace is quite expired, yet they ought to deeply apprehend the danger, lest it should expire before their necessary work be done and their peace made. For tho it can be of no use for them to know the former, and therefore they have no means appointed them by which to know it, 'tis of great use to apprehend the latter; and they have sufficient ground for the apprehension. All the cautions and warnings wherewith the Holy Spirit abounds, of the kind with those already mentioned, have that manifest design. And nothing can be more important, or opposite to this purpose, than that solemn charge of the great apostle: "Work out your own salvation with fear and trembling"; considered together with the subjoined ground of it; "For it is God that worketh in you to will and to do of his own good pleasure." How correspondent is the one with the other; work for He works: there were no working at all to any purpose, or with any hope, if He did not work. And work with fear and trembling, for He works of His own good pleasure, q.d., "'Twere the greatest folly imaginable to trifle with One that works at so perfect liberty, under no obligation, that may desist when He will; to impose upon so absolutely sovereign and arbitrary an Agent, that owes you nothing; and from whose former gracious operations not complied with you can draw no argument, unto any following ones, that because He doth, therefore He will. As there is no certain connection between present time and future, but all time is made up of undepending, not strictly coherent, moments, so as no man can be sure, because one now exists, another shall; there is also no more certain connection between the arbitrary acts of a free agent within such time; so that I can not be sure, because He now darts in light upon me, is now convincing me, now awakening me, therefore He will still do so, again and again." Upon this ground then, what exhortation could be more proper than this? "Work out your salvation with fear and trembling." What could be more awfully monitory and enforcing of it than that He works only of mere good will and pleasure? How should I tremble to think, if I should be negligent, or undutiful, He may give out the next moment, may let the work fall, and me perish? And there is more especial cause for such an apprehension upon the concurrence of such things as these:

1. If the workings of God's Spirit upon the soul of a man have been more than ordinarily strong and urgent, and do not now cease: if there have been more powerful convictions, deeper humiliations, more awakened fears, more formed purposes of a new life, more fervent desires that are now vanished, and the

sinner returns to his dead and dull temper.

2. If there be no disposition to reflect and consider the difference, no sense of his loss, but he apprehends such workings of spirit in him unnecessary troubles to him, and thinks it well he is delivered and eased of them.

3. If in the time when he was under such workings of the Spirit he had made known his case to his minister, or any godly friend, whose company he now shuns, as not willing to be put in mind, or hear any more of such matters.

4. If, hereupon he hath more indulged sensual inclination, taken more liberty, gone against the check of his own conscience, broken former good resolutions, involved himself in the guilt of any grosser sins.

5. If conscience, so baffled, be now silent, lets him alone, grows more sluggish and weaker, which it must as his lusts grow stronger.

6. If the same lively, powerful ministry which before affected him much, now moves him not.

7. If especially he is grown into a dislike of such preaching—if serious godliness, and what tends to it, are become distasteful to him—if discourses of God, and of Christ, of death and judgment, and of a holy life, are reckoned superflous and needless, are unsavory and disrelished—if he have learned to put disgraceful names upon things of this import, and the persons that most value them live accordingly—if he hath taken the seat of the scorner, and makes it his business to deride what he had once a reverence for, or took some complacency in.

8. If, upon all this, God withdraw such a ministry, so that he is now warned, admonished, exhorted and striven with, as formerly, no more. Oh, the fearful danger of that man's case! Hath he no cause to fear lest the things of his peace should be forever hid from his eyes? Surely he hath much cause of fear, but mot of despair. Fear in this case would be his great duty, and might yet prove the means of saving him—despair would be his very heinous and destroying sin. If yet he would be stirred up to

consider his case, whence he is fallen, and whither he is falling, and set himself to serious seekings of God, cast down himself before Him, abase himself, cry for mercy as for his life, there is yet hope in his case. God may make here an instance what He can obtain of Himself to do for a perishing wretch. But if with any that have lived under the gospel, their day is quite expired, and the things of their peace now forever hid from their eyes, this is in itself a most deplorable case, and much lamented by our Lord Jesus Himself. That the case is in itself most deplorable, who sees not? A soul lost! a creature capable of God! upon its way to Him! near to the kingdom of God! shipwrecked in the port! Oh, sinner, from how high a hope art thou fallen! into what depths of misery and we! And that it was lamented by our Lord is in the text. He beheld the city (very generally, we have reason to apprehend, inhabited by such wretched creatures) and wept over it. This was a very affectionate lamentation. We lament often, very heartily, many a sad case for which we do not shed tears. But tears, such tears, falling from such eyes! the issues of the purest and best-governed passion that ever was, showed the true greatness of the cause. Here could be no exorbitancy or unjust excess, nothing more than was proportional to the occasion. There needs no other proof that this is a sad case than that our Lord lamented it with tears, which that He did we are plainly told, so that, touching that, there is no place for doubt. All that is liable to question is, whether we are to conceive in Him any like resentments of such cases, in His present glorified state? Indeed, we can not think heaven a place or state of sadness or lamentation, and must take heed of conceiving anything there, especially on the throne of glory, unsuitable to the most perfect nature, and the most glorious state. We are not to imagine tears there, which, in that happy region are wiped away from inferior eyes—no grief, sorrow, or sighing, which are all fled away, and shall be no more, as there can be no other turbid passion of any kind. But when expressions that import anger or grief are used, even concerning God Himself, we must sever in our conception everything of imperfection, and ascribe everything of real perfection. We are not to think such expressions signify nothing, that they have no meaning, or that nothing at all is to be attributed to Him under them. Nor are we again to think they signify the same thing with what we find in ourselves, and are wont to express by those names. In the divine nature there may be real, and yet most serene, complacency and displacency—viz., that, unaccompanied by the least commotion, that impart nothing of imperfection, but perfection rather, as it is a perfection to apprehend things suitably to what in themselves they are. The holy Scriptures frequently speak of God as angry, and grieved for the sins of men, and their miseries which ensue therefrom. And a real aversion and dislike is signified thereby, and by many other expressions, which in us would signify vehement agitations of affection, that we are sure can have no place in Him. We ought, therefore, in our own thoughts to ascribe to Him that calm aversion of will, in reference to the sins and miseries of men in general; and in our own apprehensions to remove to the utmost distance from Him all such agitations of passion or affection, even tho some expressions that occur carry a great appearance thereof, should they be understood according to human measures, as they are human forms of speech. As, to instance in what is said by the glorious God Himself, and very near in sense to what we have in the text, what can be more pathetic than that lamenting wish, "Oh, that my people had hearkened unto me, and Israel had walked in my ways!" But we must take heed lest, under the pretense that we can not ascribe everything to God that such expressions seem to import, we therefore ascribe nothing. We ascribe nothing, if we do not ascribe a real unwillingness that men should sin on, and perish, and consequently a real willingness that they should turn to Him, and live, which so many plain texts assert. And therefore it is unavoidably imposed upon us to believe that God is truly unwilling of some things which He doth not think fit to interpose His omnipotency to hinder, and is truly willing of some things which He doth not put forth His omnipotency to effect.

We can not, therefore, doubt but that,

1. He distinctly comprehends the truth of any such case. He beholds, from the throne of His glory above, all the treaties which are held and managed with sinners in His name, and what their deportments are therein. His eyes are as a flame of fire, wherewith He searcheth hearts and trieth reins. He hath seen therefore, sinner, all along every time an offer of grace hath been made to thee, and been rejected; when thou hast slighted counsels and warnings that have been given thee, exhortations and treaties that have been prest upon thee for many years together, and how thou hast hardened thy heart against reproofs and threatenings, against promises and allurements, and beholds the tendency of all this, what is like to come to it, and that, if thou persist, it will be bitterness in the end.

2. That He hath a real dislike of the sinfulness of thy course. It is not indifferent to Him whether thou obeyest or disobeyest the gospel, whether thou turn and repent or no; that He is truly displeased at thy trifling, sloth, negligence, impenitency, hardness of heart, stubborn obstinacy, and contempt of His grace, and takes real offense at them.

3. He hath real kind propensions toward thee, and is ready to receive thy returning soul, and effectually to mediate with the offended majesty of Heaven for thee, as long as there is any hope in thy case.

4. When He sees there is no hope, He pities thee, while thou seest it not, and dost not pity thyself. Pity and mercy above are not names only; 'tis a great reality that is signified by them, and that hath place here in far higher excellency and perfection than it can with us poor mortals here below. Ours is but borrowed and participated from that first fountain and original above. Thou dost not perish unlamented even with the purest heavenly pity, tho thou hast made thy case incapable of remedy; as the well tempered judge bewails the sad end of the malefactor, whom justice obliges him not to spare or save.

And that thou mayst not throw away thy soul and so great a hope, through mere sloth and loathness to be at some pains for thy life, let the text, which hath been thy directory about the things that belong to thy peace, be also thy motive, as it gives thee to behold the Son of God weeping over such as would not know those things. Shall not the Redeemer's tears move thee? O hard heart! Consider what these tears import to this purpose.

1. They signify the real depth and greatness of the misery into which thou are falling. They drop from an intellectual and most comprehensive eye, that sees far and pierces deep into things, hath a wide and large prospect; takes the comfort of that forlorn state into which unreconcilable sinners are hastening, in all the horror of it. The Son of God did not weep vain and causeless tears, or for a light matter; nor did He for Himself either spend His own or desire the profusion of others' tears. "Weep not for me, O daughters of Jerusalem," etc. He knows the value of souls, the weight of guilt, and how low it will press and sink them; the severity of God's justice and the power of His anger, and what the fearful effects of them will be when they finally fall. If thou understandest not these things thyself, believe Him that did; at least believe His tears.

2. They signify the sincerity of His love and pity, the truth and tenderness of His compassion. Canst thou think His deceitful tears? His, who never knew guile? Was this like the rest of His course? And remember that He who shed tears did, from the same fountain of love and mercy, shed blood too! Was that also done to deceive? Thou makest thyself a very considerable thing indeed, if thou thinkest the Son of God counted it worth His while to weep, and bleed, and die, to deceive thee into a false esteem of Him and His love. But if it be the greatest madness imaginable to entertain any such thought but that His tears were sincere and unartificial, the natural, genuine expression of undissembled benignity and pity, thou art then to consider what love and compassion thou art now sinning against; what bowels thou spurnest; and that if thou perishest, 'tis under such guilt as

the devils themselves are not liable to, who never had a Redeemer bleeding for them, nor, that we ever find, weeping over them.

3. They show the remedilessness of thy case if thou persist in impenitency and unbelief till the things of thy peace be quite hid from thine eyes. These tears will then be the last issues of (even defeated) love, of love that is frustrated of its kind design. Thou mayst perceive in these tears the steady, unalterable laws of heaven, the inflexibleness of the divine justice, that holds thee in adamantine bonds, and hath sealed thee up, if thou prove incurably obstinate and impenitent, unto perdition; so that even the Redeemer Himself, He that is mighty to save, can not at length save thee, but only weep over thee, drop tears into thy flame, which assuage it not; but (tho they have another design, even to express true compassion) do yet unavoidably heighten and increase the fervor of it, and will do so to all eternity. He even tells thee, sinner, "Thou hast despised My blood; thou shalt yet have My tears." That would have saved thee, these do only lament thee lost. But the tears wept over others, as lost and past hope, why should they not yet melt thee, while as yet there is hope in thy case? If thou be effectually melted in thy very soul, and looking to Him whom thou hast pierced, dost truly mourn over Him, thou mayst assure thyself the prospect His weeping eye had of lost souls did not include thee. His weeping over thee would argue thy case forlorn and hopeless; thy mourning over Him will make it safe and happy. That it may be so, consider, further, that,

4. They signify how very intent He is to save souls, and how gladly He would save thine, if yet thou wilt accept of mercy while it may be had. For if He weep over them that will not be saved, from the same love that is the spring of these tears, would saving mercies proceed to those that are become willing to receive them. And that love that wept over them that were lost, how will it glory in them that are saved! There His love is disappointed and vexed, crossed in its gracious intendment; but here, having compassed it, how will He joy over thee with singing, and rest

in His love! And thou also, instead of being revolved in a like ruin with the unreconciled sinners of old Jerusalem, shalt be enrolled among the glorious citizens of the new, and triumph together with them in glory.

BOURDALOUE

THE PASSION OF CHRIST

BIOGRAPHICAL NOTE

Louis Bourdaloue was born at Bourges, in 1632. At the age of sixteen he entered the order of the Jesuits and was thoroughly educated in the scholarship, philosophy and theology of the day. He devoted himself entirely to the work of preaching, and was ten times called upon to address Louis XIV and his court from the pulpit as Bossuet's successor. This was an unprecedented record and yet Bourdaloue could adapt his style to any audience, and "mechanics left their shops, merchants their business, and lawyers their court house" to hear him. His high personal character, his simplicity of life, his clear, direct, and logical utterance as an accomplished orator united to make him not only "the preacher of kings but the king of preachers." Retiring from the pulpit late in life he ministered to the sick and to prisoners. He died in Paris, 1704.

BOURDALOUE

1632-1704
THE PASSION OF CHRIST

And there followed him a great company of people, and of women, which also bewailed and lamented him. But Jesus turning unto them, said, "Daughters of Jerusalem, weep not for me, but weep for your selves, and for your children."—Luke xxiii., 27, 28.

The passion of Jesus Christ, however sorrowful and ignominious it may appear to us, must nevertheless have been to Jesus Christ Himself an object of delight, since this God-man, by a wonderful secret of His wisdom and love, has willed that the mystery of it shall be continued and solemnly renewed in His Church until the final consummation of the world. For what is the Eucharist but a perpetual repetition of the Savior's passion, and what has the Savior supposed in instituting it, but that whatever passed at Calvary is not only represented but consummated on our altars? That is to say, that He is still performing the functions of the victim anew, and is every moment virtually sacrificed, as tho it were not sufficient that He should have suffered once; at least that His love, as powerful as it is free, has given to His adorable sufferings that character of perpetuity which they have in the Sacrament, and which renders them so salutary to us. Behold, Christians, what the love of God has devised; but behold, also, what has happened through the malice of men! At the same time that Jesus Christ, in the sacrament of His body, repeats His holy passion in a manner altogether mysterious, men, the false imitators, or rather base corrupters of the works of God, have found means to renew this same passion, not only in a profane, but in a criminal, sacrilegious, and horrible manner!

Do not imagine that I speak figuratively. Would to God, Christians, that what I am going to say to you were only a figure, and that you were justified in vindicating yourselves to-day against the horrible expressions which I am obliged to employ! I speak in the literal sense, and you ought to be more affected with this discourse, if what I advance appears to you to be overcharged; for it is by your excesses that it is so, and not by my words. Yes, my dear hearers, the sinners of the age, by the disorders of their lives, renew the bloody and tragic passion of the Son of God in the world; I will venture to say that the sinners of the age cause to the Son of God, even in the state of glory, as many new passions as they have committed outrages against Him by their actions! Apply yourselves to form an idea of them; and in this picture, which will surprize you, recognize what you are, that you may weep bitterly over yourselves! What do we see in the passion of Jesus Christ? A divine Savior betrayed and abandoned by cowardly disciples, persecuted by pontiffs and hypocritical priests, ridiculed and mocked in the palace of Herod by impious courtiers, placed upon a level with Barabbas, and to whom Barabbas is preferred by a blind and inconstant people, exposed to the insults of libertinism, and treated as a mock king by a troop of soldiers equally barbarous and insolent; in fine, crucified by merciless executioners! Behold, in a few words, what is most humiliating and most cruel in the death of the Savior of the world! Then tell me if this is not precisely what we now see, of what we are every day called to be witnesses. Let us resume; and follow me.

Betrayed and abandoned by cowardly disciples; such, O divine Savior, has been Thy destiny. But it was not enough that the apostles, the first men whom Thou didst choose for Thine own, in violation of the most holy engagement, should have forsaken Thee in the last scene of Thy life; that one of them should have sold Thee, another renounced Thee, and all disgraced themselves by a flight which was, perhaps, the most sensible of all the wounds that Thou didst feel in dying. This wound must be again opened by a thousand acts of infidelity yet more scandalous. Even in the Christian ages we must see men bearing the character of Thy disciples, and not having the resolution to sustain it; Christians, prevaricators, and deserters from their faith; Christians ashamed of declaring themselves for Thee, not daring to appear what they are, renouncing at least in the exterior what they have profest, flying when they ought to fight; in a word, Christians in form, ready to follow Thee even to the Supper when in prosperity, and while it required no sacrifice, but resolved to abandon Thee in the moment of temptation. It is on your account, and my own, my dear hearers, that I speak, and behold what ought to be the subject of our sorrow.

A Savior mortally persecuted by pontiffs and hypocritical priests! Let us not enter, Christians, into the discussion of this article, at which your piety would, perhaps, be offended, and which would weaken or prejudice the respect which you owe to the ministers of the Lord. It belongs to us, my brethren, to meditate to-day on this fact in the spirit of holy compunction; to us consecrated to the ministry of the altars, to us priests of Jesus Christ, whom God has chosen in His Church to be the dispensers of His sacraments. It does not become me to remonstrate in this place. God forbid that I should undertake to judge those who sustain the sacred office! This is not the duty of humility to which my condition calls me. Above all, speaking as I do, before many ministers, the irreprehensible life of whom contributes so much to the edification of the people, I am not yet so infatuated as to make myself the judge, much less the censor of their conduct.

But tho it should induce you only to acknowledge the favors with which God prevents you, as a contrast, from the frightful blindness into which He permits others to fall, remember that the priests and the princes of the priests, are those whom the evangelist describes as the authors of the conspiracy formed against the Savior of the world, and of the wickedness committed against Him. Remember that this scandal is notoriously public, and renewed still every day in Christianity. Remember, but with fear and horror, that the greatest persecutors of Jesus Christ are not lay libertines, but wicked priests; and that among the wicked priests, those whose corruption and iniquity are covered with the veil of hypocrisy are His most dangerous and most cruel enemies. A hatred, disguised under the name of zeal, and covered with the specious pretext of observance of the law, was the first movement of the persecution which the Pharisees and the priests raised against the Son of God. Let us fear lest the same passion should blind us! Wretched passion, exclaims St. Bernard, which spreads the venom of its malignity even over the most lovely of the children of men, and which could not see a God upon earth without hating Him! A hatred not only of the prosperity and happiness, but what is yet more strange, of the merit and perfection of others! A cowardly and shameful passion, which, not content with having caused the death of Jesus Christ, continues to persecute Him by rending His mystical body, which is the Church; dividing His members, which are believers; and stifling in their hearts that charity which is the spirit of Christianity! Behold, my brethren, the subtle temptation against which we have to defend ourselves, and under which it is but too common for us to fall!

A Redeemer reviled and mocked in the palace of Herod by the impious creatures of his court! This was, without doubt, one of the most sensible insults which Jesus Christ received. But do not suppose, Christians, that this act of impiety ended there. It has passed from the court of Herod, from that prince destitute of religion, into those even of Christian princes. And is not the Savior still a subject of ridicule to the libertine spirits which compose them? They worship Him externally, but internally how do they regard His maxims? What idea have they of His humility, of His poverty, of His sufferings? Is not virtue either unknown or despised? It is not a rash zeal which induces me to speak in this manner; it is what you too often witness, Christians; it is what you perhaps feel in yourselves; and a little reflection upon the manners of the court will convince you that there is nothing that I say which is not confirmed by a thousand examples, and that you yourselves are sometimes unhappy accomplices in these crimes.

Herod had often earnestly wished to see Jesus Christ. The reputation which so many miracles had given Him, excited the curiosity of this prince, and he did not doubt but that a man who commanded all nature might strike some wonderful blow to escape from the persecution of His enemies. But the Son of God, who had not been sparing of His prodigies for the salvation of others, spared them for Himself, and would not say a single word about His own safety. He considered Herod and his people as profane persons, with whom he thought it improper to hold any intercourse, and he preferred rather to pass for a fool than to satisfy the false wisdom of the world. As His kingdom was not of this world, as He said to Pilate, it was not at the court that He designed to establish Himself. He knew too well that His doctrine could not be relished in a place where the rules of worldly wisdom only were followed, and where all the miracles which He had performed had not been sufficient to gain men full of love for themselves and intoxicated with their greatness. In this corrupted region they breathe only the air of vanity; they esteem only that which is splendid; they speak only of preferment: and on whatever side we cast our eyes, we see nothing but what either flatters or inflames the ambitious desires of the heart of man.

What probability then was there that Jesus Christ, the most humble of all men, should obtain a hearing where only pageantry and pride prevail! If He had been surrounded with honors and riches, He would have found partisans near Herod and in every other place. But as He preached a renunciation of the world both to His disciples and to Himself, let us not be astonished that they treated Him with so much disdain. Such is the prediction of the holy man Job, and which after Him must be accomplished in the person of all the righteous; "the upright man is laughed to scorn." In fact, my dear hearers, you know that, whatever virtue and merit we may possess, they are not enough to procure us esteem at court. Enter it, and appear only like Jesus Christ, clothed with the robe of innocence; only walk with Jesus Christ in the way of simplicity; only speak as Jesus Christ to render testimony to the truth, and you will find that you meet with no better treatment there than Jesus Christ. To be well received there, you must have pomp and splendor. To keep your station there, you must have artifice and intrigue. To be favorably heard there, you must have complaisance and flattery. Then all this is opposed to Jesus Christ; and the court being what it is—that is to say, the kingdom of the prince of this world—it is not surprizing that the kingdom of Jesus Christ can not be established there. But wo to you, princes of the earth! Wo to you, men of the world, who despise this incarnate wisdom, for you shall be despised in your turn, and the contempt which shall fall upon you shall be much more terrible than the contempt which you manifest can be prejudicial.

A Savior placed upon a level with Barabbas, and to whom Barabbas is preferred by a blind and fickle rabble! How often have we been guilty of the same outrage against Jesus Christ as the blind and fickle Jews! How often, after having received Him in triumph in the sacrament of the communion, seduced by cupidity, have we not preferred either a pleasure or interest after which we sought, in violation of His law, to this God of glory! How often divided between conscience which governed us, and passion which corrupted us, have we not renewed this abominable judgment, this unworthy preference of the creature even above our God! Christians, observe this application; it is that of St. Chrysostom, and if you properly understand it, you must be affected by it. Conscience, which, in spite of ourselves, presides in us as judge, said inwardly to us, "What art thou going to do? Behold thy pleasure on the one hand, and thy God on the other: for which of the two dost thou declare thyself? for thou canst not save both; thou must either lose thy pleasure or thy God; and it is for thee to decide." And the passion, which by a monstrous infidelity had acquired the influence over our hearts, made us conclude—I will keep my pleasure. "But what then will become of thy God," replied conscience secretly, "and what must I do, I, who can not prevent myself from maintaining His interests against thee?" I care not what will become of my God, answered passion insolently; I will satisfy myself, and the resolution is taken. "But dost thou know," proceeded conscience by its remorse, "that in indulging thyself in this pleasure it will at last submit thy Savior to death and crucifixion for thee?" It is of no consequence if He be crucified, provided I can have my enjoyments. "But what evil has He done, and what reason hast thou to abandon Him in this manner?" My pleasure is my reason; and since Christ is the enemy of my pleasure, and my pleasure crucifies Him, I say it again, let Him be crucified.

Behold, my dear hearers, what passes every day in the consciences of men, and what passes in you and in me, every time that we fall into sin, which causes death to Jesus Christ, as well as to our souls! Behold what makes the enormity and wickedness of this sin! I know that we do not always speak, that we do not always explain ourselves in such express terms and in so perceptible a manner; but after all, without explaining ourselves so distinctly and so sensibly, there is a language of the heart which says all this. For, from the moment that I know that this pleasure is criminal and forbidden of God, I know that it is impossible for me to desire it, impossible to seek it, without losing God; and consequently I prefer this pleasure to God in the desire that I form of it, and in the pursuit that I make after it. This, then, is sufficient to justify the thought of St. Chrysostom and the doctrine of the theologians upon the nature of deadly sin ...

That there are men, and Christian men, to whom, by a secret judgment of God, the passion of Jesus Christ, salutary as it is, may become useless, is a truth too essential in our religion to be unknown, and too sorrowful not to be the subject of our grief. When the Savior from the height of His cross, ready to give up His spirit, raised this cry toward heaven, "My God, my God, why hast thou forsaken me?" there was no one who did not suppose but that the violence of His torments forced from Him this complaint, and perhaps we ourselves yet believe it. But the great Bishop Arnauld de Chartres, penetrating deeper into the thoughts and affections of this dying Savior, says, with much more reason, that the complaint of Christ Jesus to His Father proceeded from the sentiment with which He was affected, in representing to Himself the little fruit which His death would produce; in considering the small number of the elect who would profit by it; in foreseeing with horror the infinite number of the reprobate, for whom it would be useless: as if He had wished to proclaim that His merits were not fully enough nor worthily enough remunerated; and that after having done so much work He had a right to promise to Himself a different success in behalf of men. The words of this author are admirable: Jesus Christ complains, says this learned prelate, but of what does He complain? That the wickedness of sinners makes Him lose what ought to be the reward of the conflicts which He has maintained; that millions of the human race for whom He suffers will, nevertheless, be excluded from the benefit of redemption. And because He regards Himself in them as their head, and themselves, in spite of their worthlessness, as the members of His mystical body; seeing them abandoned by God, He complains of being abandoned Himself: "My God, my God, why hast thou forsaken me?" He complains of what made St. Paul groan when, transported with an apostolic zeal, he said to the Galatians: "What, my brethren, is Jesus Christ then dead in vain? Is the mystery of the cross then nothing to you? Will not this blood which He has so abundantly shed have the virtue to sanctify you?"

But here, Christians, I feel myself affected with a thought which, contrary as it appears to that of the apostle, only serves to strengthen and confirm it. For it appears that St. Paul is grieved because Jesus Christ has suffered in vain; but I, I should almost console myself if He had only suffered in vain, and if His passion was only rendered useless to us. That which fills me with consternation is, that at the same time that we render it useless to ourselves, by an inevitable necessity it must become pernicious; for this passion, says St. Gregory of Nazianzen, "partakes of the nature of those remedies which, kill if they do not heal, and of which the effect is either to give life or to convert itself into poison; lose nothing of this, I beseech you." Remember, then, Christians, what happened during the judgment and at the moment of the condemnation of the Son of God.

When Pilate washed his hands before the Jews and declared to them that there was nothing worthy of death in this righteous man, but that the crime from which he freed himself rested upon them, and that they would have to answer for it, they all cried with one voice that they consented to it, and that they readily agreed that the blood of this just man should fall upon them and upon their children. You know what this cry has cost them. You know the curses which one such imprecation has drawn upon them, the anger of heaven which began from that time to burst upon this nation, the ruin of Jerusalem which followed soon after—the carnage of their citizens, the profanation of their temple, the destruction of their republic, the visible character of their reprobation which their unhappy posterity bear to this day, that universal banishment, that exile of sixteen hundred years, that slavery through all the earth—and all in consequence of the authentic prediction which Jesus Christ made to them of it when going to Calvary, and with circumstances which incontestably prove that a punishment as exemplary as this can not be imputed but to decide which they had committed in the person of the Savior; since it is evident, says St. Augustine, that the Jews were never further from idolatry nor more religious observers of their law than they were then, and that, excepting the crime of the death of Jesus Christ, God, very far from punishing them, would, it seems, rather have loaded them with His blessings. You know all this, I say; and all this is a convincing proof that the blood of this God-man is virtually fallen upon these sacrilegious men, and that God, in condemning them by their own mouth, altho in spite of Himself, employs that to destroy them which was designed for their salvation.

But, Christians, to speak with the Holy Spirit, this has happened to the Jews only as a figure; it is only the shadow of the fearful curses of which the abuse of the merits and passion of the Son of God must be to us the source and the measure. I will explain myself. What do we, my dear hearers, when borne away by the immoderate desires of our hearts to a sin against which our consciences protest? And what do we, when, possest of the spirit of the world, we resist a grace which solicits us, which presses us to obey God? Without thinking upon it, and without wishing it, we secretly pronounce the same sentence of death which the Jews pronounced against themselves before Pilate, when they said to him, "His blood be upon us." For this grace which we despise is the price of the blood of Jesus Christ, and the sin that we commit is an actual profanation of this very blood. It is, then, as if we were to say to God: "Lord, I clearly see what engagement I make, and I know what risk I run, but rather than not satisfy my own desires, I consent that the blood of Thy Son shall fall upon me. This will be to bear the chastisement of it, but I will indulge my passion; Thou hast a right to draw forth from it a just indignation, but nevertheless I will complete my undertaking."

Thus we condemn ourselves. And here, Christians, is one of the essential foundations of this terrible mystery of the eternity of the punishment with which faith threatens us, and against which our reason revolts. We suppose that we can not have any knowledge of it in this life, and we are not aware, says St. Chrysostom, that we find it completely in the blood of the Savior, or rather in our profanation of it every day. For this blood, my brethren, adds this holy doctor, is enough to make eternity not less frightful, but less incredible. And behold the reason: This blood is of an infinite dignity; it can therefore be avenged only by an infinite punishment. This blood, if we destroy ourselves, will cry eternally against us at the tribunal of God. It will eternally excite the wrath of God against us. This blood, falling upon lost souls, will fix a stain upon them, which shall never be effaced. Their torments must consequently never end.

A reprobate in hell will always appear in the eyes of God stained with that blood which he has so basely treated. God will then always abhor him; and, as the aversion of God from His creature is that which makes hell, it must be inferred that hell will be eternal. And in this, O my God, Thou art sovereignly just, sovereignly holy, and worthy of our praise and adoration. It is in this way that the beloved disciple declared it even to God Himself in the Apocalypse. Men, said he, have shed the blood of Thy servants and of Thy prophets; therefore they deserve to drink it, and to drink it from the cup of Thine indignation. "For they have shed the blood of saints and prophets, and thou hast given them blood to drink." An expression which the Scripture employs to describe the extreme infliction of divine vengeance. Ah! if the blood of the prophets has drawn down the scourge of God upon men, what may we not expect from the blood of Jesus Christ? If the blood of martyrs is heard crying out in heaven against the persecutors of the faith, how much more will the blood of the Redeemer be heard!

Then once more, Christians, behold the deplorable necessity to which we are reduced. This blood which flows from Calvary either demands grace for us, or justice against us. When we apply ourselves to it by a lively faith and a sincere repentance, it demands grace; but when by our disorders and impieties we check its salutary virtue, it demands justice, and it infallibly obtains it. It is in this blood, says St. Bernard, that all righteous souls are purified; but by a prodigy exactly opposite, it is also in this same blood that all the sinners of the land defile themselves, and render themselves, if I may use the expression, more hideous in the sight of God.

Ah! my God, shall I eternally appear in thine eyes polluted with that blood which washes away the crimes of others? If I had simply to bear my own sins, I might promise myself a punishment less rigorous, considering my sins as my misfortune, my weakness, my ignorance. Then, perhaps, Thou wouldst be less offended on account of them. But when these sins with which I shall be covered shall present themselves before me as so many sacrileges with respect to the blood of Thy Son; when the abuse of this blood shall be mixed and confounded with all the disorders of my life; when there shall not be one of them against which this blood shall not cry louder than the blood of Abel against Cain; then, O God of my soul I what will become of me in thy presence? No, Lord, cries the same St. Bernard affectionately, suffer not the blood of my Savior to fall upon me in this manner. Let it fall upon me to sanctify, but let it not fall upon me to destroy. Let it fall upon me in a right use of the favors which are the divine overflowings of it, and not through the blindness of mind and hardness of heart which are the most terrible punishments of it. Let it fall upon me by the participation of the sacred Eucharist, which is the precious source of it, and not by the maledictions attached to the despisers of Thy sacraments. In fine, let it fall upon me by influencing my conduct and inducing the practise of good works, and let it not fall upon me for my wanderings, my infidelities, my obstinacy, and my impenitence. This, my brethren, is what we ought to ask to-day from Jesus Christ crucified. It is with these views that we ought to go to the foot of the cross and catch the blood as it flows. He was the Savior of the Jews as well as ours, but this Savior, St. Augustine says, the Jews have converted into their judge. Avert from us such an evil. May He Who died to save us be our Savior. May He be our Savior during all the days of our lives. And may His merits, shed upon us abundantly, lose none of their efficacy in our hands, but be preserved entire by the fruits we produce from them. May He be our Savior in death. And at the last moment may the cross be our support, and thus may He consummate the work of our salvation which He has begun. May He be our Savior in a blest eternity, where we shall be as much the sharer in His glory as we have been in His sufferings.

FÉNELON

THE SAINTS CONVERSE WITH GOD

BIOGRAPHICAL NOTE

François de Salignac de La Mothe-Fénelon, Archbishop of Cambray, and private tutor to the heir-apparent of France, was born of a noble family in Perigord, 1651. In 1675 he received holy orders, and soon afterward made the acquaintance of Bossuet, whom he henceforth looked up to as his master. It was the publication of his "De l'Éducation des Filles" that brought him his first fame, and had some influence in securing his appointment in 1689 to be preceptor of the Duke of Burgundy. In performing this office he thought it necessary to compose his own text-books, such as would teach the vanity of worldly greatness and the loftiness of virtue. He was promoted to the archbishopric of Cambray in 1695, and subsequently became entangled in the religious aberrations of Madame Guyon. Fénelon came into controversy with Bossuet, whose severity against his friend was rebuked by the Pope, who, nevertheless, condemned some of the Archbishop of Cambray's views. Fénelon submitted, and withdrew to his diocesan see, where he died in 1715. His deep spirituality and eloquence are exemplified in the following sermon.

FÉNELON

1651-1715
THE SAINTS CONVERSE WITH GOD

Pray without ceasing.—I Thess. v., 17

Of all the duties enjoined by Christianity none is more essential, and yet more neglected, than prayer. Most people consider this exercise a wearisome ceremony, which they are justified in abridging as much as possible. Even those whose profession or fears lead them to pray, do it with such languor and wanderings of mind that their prayers, far from drawing down blessings, only increase their condemnation. I wish to demonstrate, in this discourse, first, the general necessity of prayer; secondly, its peculiar duty; thirdly, the manner in which we ought to pray.

First. God alone can instruct us in our duty. The teachings of men, however wise and well disposed they may be, are still ineffectual, if God do not shed on the soul that light which opens the mind to truth. The imperfections of our fellow creatures cast a shade over the truths that we learn from them. Such is our weakness that we do not receive, with sufficient docility, the instructions of those who are as imperfect as ourselves. A thousand suspicions, jealousies, fears, and prejudices prevent us from profiting, as we might, by what we hear from men; and tho they announce the most serious truths, yet what they do weakens the effect of what they say. In a word, it is God alone who can perfectly teach us.

St. Bernard said, in writing to a pious friend—If you are seeking less to satisfy a vain curiosity than to get true wisdom, you will sooner find it in deserts than in books. The silence of the rocks and the pathless forests will teach you better than the eloquence of the most gifted men. "All," says St. Augustine, "that we possess of truth and wisdom is a borrowed good flowing from that fountain for which we ought to thirst in the fearful desert of this world, that, being refreshed and invigorated by these dews from heaven, we may not faint upon the road that conducts us to a better country. Every attempt to satisfy the cravings of our hearts at other sources only increases the void. You will be always poor if you do not possess the only true riches." All light that does not proceed from God is false; it only dazzles us; it sheds no illumination upon the difficult paths in which we must walk, along the precipices that are about us.

Our experience and our reflections can not, on all occasions, give us just and certain rules of conduct. The advice of our wisest, and most sincere friends is not always sufficient; many things escape their observation, and many that do not are too painful to be spoken. They suppress much from delicacy, or sometimes from a fear of transgressing the bounds that our friendship and confidence in them will allow. The animadversions of our enemies, however severe or vigilant they may be, fail to enlighten us with regard to ourselves. Their malignity furnishes our self-love with a pretext for the indulgence of the greatest faults. The blindness of our self-love is so great that we find reasons for being satisfied with ourselves, while all the world condemn us. What must we learn from all this darkness? That it is God alone who can dissipate it; that it is He alone whom we can never doubt; that He alone is true, and knoweth all things; that if we go to Him in sincerity, He will teach us what men dare not tell us, what books can not—all that is essential for us to know.

Be assured that the greatest obstacle to true wisdom is the self-confidence inspired by that which is false. The first step toward this precious knowledge is earnestly to desire it, to feel the want of it, and to be convinced that they who seek it must address themselves to the Father of lights, who freely gives to him who asks in faith. But if it be true that God alone can enlighten us, it is not the less true that He will do this simply in answer to our prayers. Are we not happy, indeed, in being able to obtain so great a blessing by only asking for it? No part of the effort that we make to acquire the transient enjoyments of this life is necessary to obtain these heavenly blessings. What will we not do, what are we not willing to suffer, to possess dangerous and contemptible things, and often without any success? It is not thus with heavenly things. God is always ready to grant them to those who make the request in sincerity and truth. The Christian life is a long and continual tendency of our hearts toward that eternal goodness which we desire on earth. All our happiness consists in thirsting for it. Now this thirst is prayer. Ever desire to approach your Creator and you will never cease to pray.

Do not think that it is necessary to pronounce many words. To pray is to say, Let Thy will be done. It is to form a good purpose; to raise your heart to God; to lament your weakness; to sigh at the recollection of your frequent disobedience. This prayer demands neither method, nor science, nor reasoning; it is not essential to quit one's employment; it is a simple movement of the heart toward its Creator, and a desire that whatever you are doing you may do it to His glory. The best of all prayers is to act with a pure intention, and with a continual reference to the will of God. It depends much upon ourselves whether our prayers be efficacious. It is not by a miracle, but by a movement of the heart that we are benefited; by a submissive spirit. Let us believe, let us trust, let us hope, and God never will reject our prayer. Yet how many Christians do we see strangers to the privilege, aliens from God, who seldom think of Him, who never open their hearts to Him; who seek elsewhere the counsels of a false wisdom, and vain and dangerous consolations, who can not resolve to seek, in humble, fervent prayer to God, a remedy for their griefs and a true knowledge of their defects, the necessary power to conquer their vicious and perverse inclinations, and the consolations and assistance they require, that they may not be discouraged in a virtuous life.

But some will say, "I have no interest in prayer; it wearies me; my imagination is excited by sensible and more agreeable objects, and wanders in spite of me."

If neither your reverence for the great truths of religion, nor the majesty of the ever-present Deity, nor the interest of your eternal salvation, have power to arrest your mind and engage it in prayer, at least mourn with me for your infidelity; be ashamed of your weakness, and wish that your thoughts were more under your control; and desire to become less frivolous and inconstant. Make an effort to subject your mind to this discipline. You will gradually acquire habit and facility. What is now tedious will become delightful; and you will then feel, with a peace that the world can not give nor take away, that God is good. Make a courageous effort to overcome yourself. There can be no occasion that more demands it.

Secondly. The peculiar obligation of prayer. Were I to give all the proofs that the subject affords, I should describe every condition of life, that I might point out its dangers, and the necessity of recourse to God in prayer. But I will simply state that under all circumstances we have need of prayer. There is no situation in which it is possible to be placed where we have not many virtues to acquire and many faults to correct. We find in our temperament, or in our habits, or in the peculiar character of our minds, qualities that do not suit our occupations, and that oppose our duties. One person is connected by marriage to another whose temper is so unequal that life becomes a perpetual warfare. Some, who are exposed to the contagious atmosphere of the world, find themselves so susceptible to the vanity which they inhale that all their pure desires vanish. Others have solemnly promised to renounce their resentments, to conquer their aversions, to suffer with patience certain crosses, and to repress their eagerness for wealth; but nature prevails, and they are vindictive, violent, impatient, and avaricious.

Whence comes it that these resolutions are so frail? That

all these people wish to improve, desire to perform their duty toward God and man better, and yet fail? It is because our own strength and wisdom, alone, are not enough. We undertake to do everything without God; therefore we do not succeed. It is at the foot of the altar that we must seek for counsel which will aid us. It is with God that we must lay our plans of virtue and usefulness; it is He alone that can render them successful. Without Him, all our designs, however good they may appear, are only temerity and delusion. Let us then pray that we may learn what we are and what we ought to be. By this means we shall not only learn the number and the evil effects of our peculiar faults, but we shall also learn to what virtues we are called, and the way to practise them. The rays of that pure and heavenly light that visit the humble soul will beam on us and we shall feel and understand that everything is possible to those who put their whole trust in God. Thus, not only to those who live in retirement, but to those who are exposed to the agitations of the world and the excitements of business, it is peculiarly necessary, by contemplation and fervent prayer, to restore their souls to that serenity which the dissipations of life and commerce with men have disturbed. To those who are engaged in business, contemplation and prayer are much more difficult than to those who live in retirement; but it is far more necessary for them to have frequent recourse to God in fervent prayer. In the most holy occupation a certain degree of precaution is necessary.

Do not devote all your time to action, but reserve a certain portion of it for meditation upon eternity. We see Jesus Christ inviting His disciples to go apart, in a desert place, and rest awhile, after their return from the cities, where they had been to announce His religion. How much more necessary is it for us to approach the source of all virtue, that we may revive our declining faith and charity, when we return from the busy scenes of life, where men speak and act as if they had never known that there is a God! We should look upon prayer as the remedy for our weakness, the rectifier of our own faults. He who was without sin prayed constantly; how much more ought we, who are sinners, to be faithful in prayer!

Even the exercise of charity is often a snare to us. It calls us to certain occupations that dissipate the mind, and that may degenerate into mere amusement. It is for this reason that St. Chrysostom says that nothing is so important as to keep an exact proportion between the interior source of virtue and the external practise of it; else, like the foolish virgins, we shall find that the oil in our lamp is exhausted when the bridegroom comes.

The necessity we feel that God should bless our labors is another powerful motive to prayer. It often happens that all human help is vain. It is God alone that can aid us, and it does not require much faith to believe that it is less our exertions, our foresight, and our industry than the blessing of the Almighty that can give success to our wishes.

Thirdly. Of the manner in which we ought to pray. 1. We must pray with attention. God listens to the voice of the heart, not to that of the lips. Our whole heart must be engaged in prayer. It must fasten upon what it prays for; and every human object must disappear from our minds. To whom should we speak with attention if not to God? Can He demand less of us than that we should think of what we say to Him? Dare we hope that He will listen to us, and think of us, when we forget ourselves in the midst of our prayers? This attention to prayer, which it is so just to exact from Christians, may be practised with less difficulty than we imagine. It is true that the most faithful souls suffer from occasional involuntary distractions. They can not always control their imaginations, and, in the silence of their spirits, enter into the presence of God. But these unbidden wanderings of the mind ought not to trouble us; and they may conduce to our perfection even more than the most sublime and affecting prayers if we earnestly strive to overcome them, and submit with humility to this experience of our infirmity. But to dwell willingly on frivolous and worldly things during prayer, to make no effort to check the vain thoughts that intrude upon this sacred employment and come between us and the Father of our spirits—is not this choosing to live the sport of our senses, and separated from God?

2. We must also ask with faith; a faith so firm that it never falters. He who prays without confidence can not hope that his prayer will be granted. Will not God love the heart that trusts in Him? Will He reject those who bring all their treasures to Him, and repose everything upon His goodness? When we pray to God, says St. Cyprian, with entire assurance, it is Himself who has given us the spirit of our prayer. Then it is the Father listening to the words of His child; it is He who dwells in our hearts, teaching us to pray. But must we confess that this filial confidence is wanting in all our prayers? Is not prayer our resource only when all others have failed us? If we look into hearts, shall we not find that we ask of God as if we had never before received benefits from Him? Shall we not discover there a secret infidelity that renders us unworthy of His goodness? Let us tremble, lest, when Jesus Christ shall judge us, He pronounce the same reproach that He did to Peter, "O thou of little faith, wherefore didst thou doubt?"

3. We must join humility with trust. Great God, said Daniel, when we prostrate ourselves at Thy feet, we do not place our hopes for the success of our prayers upon our righteousness, but upon Thy mercy. Without this disposition in our hearts, all others, however pious they may be, can not please God. St. Augustine observes that the failure of Peter should not be attributed to insincerity in his zeal for Jesus Christ. He loved his Master in good faith; in good faith he would rather have died than have forsaken Him; but his fault lay in trusting to his own strength, to do what his own heart dictated.

It is not enough to possess a right spirit, an exact knowledge of duty, a sincere desire to perform it We must continually renew this desire, and enkindle this flame within us, at the fountain of pure and eternal light.

It is the humble and contrite heart that God will not despise.

Remark the difference which the evangelist has pointed out between the prayer of the proud and presumptuous Pharisee and the humble and penitent publican. The one relates his virtues, the other deplores his sins. The good works of the one shall be set aside, while the penitence of the other shall be accepted. It will be thus with many Christians. Sinners, vile in their own eyes, will be objects of the mercy of God; while some, who have made professions of piety, will be condemned on account of the pride and arrogance that have contaminated their good works. It will be so because these have said in their hearts, "Lord, I thank thee that I am not as other men are." They imagine themselves privileged; they pretend that they alone have penetrated the mysteries of the kingdom of God; they have a language and science of their own; they believe that their zeal can accomplish everything. Their regular lives favor their vanity; but in truth they are incapable of self-sacrifice, and they go to their devotions with their hearts full of pride and presumption. Unhappy are those who pray in this manner! Unhappy are those whose prayers do not render them more humble, more submissive, more watchful over their faults, and more willing to live in obscurity!

4. We must pray with love. It is love says St. Augustine, that asks, that seeks, that knocks, that finds, and that is faithful to what it finds. We cease to pray to God as soon as we cease to love Him, as soon as we cease to thirst for His perfections. The coldness of our love is the silence of our hearts toward God. Without this we may pronounce prayers, but we do not pray; for what shall lead us to meditate upon the laws of God if it be not the love of Him who has made these laws? Let our hearts be full of love, then, and they will pray. Happy are they who think seriously of the truths of religion; but far more happy are they who feel and love them! We must ardently desire that God will grant us spiritual blessings; and the ardor of our wishes must render us fit to receive the blessings. For if we pray only from custom, from fear, in the time of tribulation—- if we honor God only with our lips, while our hearts are far from Him—if we do

not feel a strong desire for the success of our prayers—if we feel a chilling indifference in approaching Him who is a consuming fire—if we have no zeal for His glory—if we do not feel hatred for sin, and a thirst for perfection, we can not hope for a blessing upon such heartless prayers.

5. We must pray with perseverance. The perfect heart is never weary of seeking God. Ought we to complain if God sometimes leaves us to obscurity, and doubt, and temptation? Trials purify humble souls, and they serve to expiate the faults of the unfaithful. They confound those who, even in their prayers, have flattered their cowardice and pride. If an innocent soul, devoted to God, suffer from any secret disturbance, it should be humble, adore the designs of God, and redouble its prayers and its fervor. How often do we hear those who every day have to reproach themselves with unfaithfulness toward God complain that He refuses to answer their prayers! Ought they not to acknowledge that it is their sins which have formed a thick cloud between Heaven and them, and that God has justly hidden Himself from them? How often has He recalled us from our wanderings! How often, ungrateful as we are, have we been deaf to His voice and insensible to His goodness! He would make us feel that we are blind and miserable when we forsake Him. He would teach us, by privation, the value of the blessings that we have slighted. And shall we not bear our punishment with patience? Who can boast of having done all that he ought to have done; of having repaired all his past errors; of having purified his heart, so that he may claim as a right that God should listen to his prayer? Most truly, all our pride, great as it is, would not be sufficient to inspire such presumption! If then, the Almightly do not grant our petitions, let us adore His justice, let us be silent, let us humble ourselves, and let us pray without ceasing. This humble perseverance will obtain from Him what we should never obtain by our own merit. It will make us pass happily from darkness to light; for know, says St. Augustine that God is near to us even when He appears far from us.

6. We should pray with a pure intention. We should not mingle in our prayers what is false with what is real; what is perishable with what is eternal; low and temporal interests with that which concerns our salvation. Do not seek to render God the protector of your self-love and ambition, but the promoter of your good desires. You ask for the gratification of your passions, or to be delivered from the cross, of which He knows you have need. Carry not to the foot of the altar irregular desires and indiscreet prayers. Sigh not for vain and fleeting pleasures. Open your heart to your Father in heaven, that His Spirit may enable you to ask for the true riches. How can He grant you, says St. Augustine, what you do not yourself desire to receive? You pray every day that His will may be done, and that His kingdom may come. How can you utter this prayer with sincerity when you prefer your own will to His, and make His law yield to the vain pretexts with which your self-love seeks to elude it? Can you make this prayer—you who disturb His reign in your heart by so many impure and vain desires? You, in fine, who fear the coming of His reign, and do not desire that God should grant what you seem to pray for? No! If He, at this moment, were to offer to give you a new heart, and render you humble, and willing to bear the cross, your pride would revolt, and you would not accept the offer; or you would make a reservation in favor of your ruling passion, and try to accommodate your piety to your humor and fancies!

SOUTH

THE IMAGE OF GOD IN MAN

BIOGRAPHICAL NOTE

Robert South, who was born in the borough of Hackney, London, England, in 1638, attracted wide attention by his vigorous mind and his clear, argumentative style in preaching. Some of his sermons are notable specimens of pulpit eloquence. A keen analytical mind, great depth of feeling, and wide range of fancy combined to make him a powerful and impressive speaker. By some critics his style has been considered unsurpassed in force and beauty. What he lacked in tenderness was made up in masculine strength. He was a born satirist. Henry Rogers said of him: "Of all the English preachers, South seems to furnish, in point of style, the truest specimens of pulpit eloquence. His robust intellect, his shrewd common sense, his vehement feelings, and a fancy always more distinguished by force than by elegance, admirably qualified him for a powerful public speaker." South became prebendary of Westminster in 1663, canon at Oxford in 1670, and rector of Islip in 1678. An edition of his writings was published in 1823. He died in 1716.

SOUTH

1638-1716
THE IMAGE OF GOD IN MAN

So God created man in his own image, in the image of God created he him.—Genesis i., 27.

How hard it is for natural reason to discover a creation before revealed, or, being revealed, to believe it, the strange opinions of the old philosophers, and the infidelity of modern atheists, is too sad a demonstration. To run the world back to its first original and infancy, and, as it were, to view nature in its cradle, and trace the outgoings of the Ancient of Days in the first instance and specimen of His creative power, is a research too great for any mortal inquiry; and we might continue our scrutiny to the end of the world, before natural reason would be able to find out when it began.

Epicurus's discourse concerning the original of the world is so fabulous and ridiculously merry that we may well judge the design of his philosophy to have been pleasure, and not instruction. Aristotle held that it streamed by connatural result and emanation from God, the infinite and eternal Mind, as the light issues from the sun; so that there was no instant of duration assignable of God's eternal existence in which the world did not also coexist. Others held a fortuitous concourse of atoms—but all seem jointly to explode a creation, still beating upon this ground, that the producing something out of nothing is impossible and incomprehensible; incomprehensible, indeed, I grant, but not therefore impossible. There is not the least transaction of sense and motion in the whole man, but philosophers are at a loss to comprehend, I am sure they are to explain it. Wherefore it is not always rational to measure the truth of an assertion by the standard of our apprehension.

But, to bring things even to the bare preception of reason, I appeal to any one who shall impartially reflect upon the ideas and conceptions of his own mind, whether he doth not find it as easy and suitable to his natural notions to conceive that an infinite Almighty power might produce a thing out of nothing, and make that to exist *de novo*, which did not exist before, as to conceive the world to have had no beginning, but to have existed from eternity, which, were it so proper for this place and exercise, I could easily demonstrate to be attended with no small train of absurdities. But then, besides that the acknowledging of a creation is safe, and the denial of it dangerous and irreligious, and yet not more, perhaps much less, demonstrable than the affirmative; so, over and above, it gives me this advantage, that, let it seem never so strange, uncouth, and incomprehensible, the nonplus of my reason will yield a fairer opportunity to my faith.

The work that I shall undertake from these words shall be to show what this image of God in man is, and wherein it doth consist. Which I shall do these two ways: 1. Negatively, by showing wherein it does not consist. 2. Positively, by showing wherein it does.

For the first of these we are to remove the erroneous opinion of the Socinians. They deny that the image of God consisted in any habitual perfections that adorned the soul of Adam, but, as to his understanding, bring him in void of all notion, a rude, unwritten blank; making him to be created as much an infant as others are born; sent into the world only to read and to spell out a God in the works of creation, to learn by degrees, till at length his understanding grew up to the stature of his body; also without any inherent habits of virtue in his will; thus divesting him of all, and stripping him of his bare essence; so that all the perfection they allowed his understanding was aptness and docility, and all that they attributed to his will was a possibility to be virtuous.

But wherein, then, according to their opinion, did this image of God consist? Why, in that power and dominion that God gave Adam over the creatures; in that he was vouched His immediate deputy upon earth, the viceroy of the creation, and lord-lieutenant of the world. But that this power and dominion is not adequately and formally the image of God, but only a part of it, is clear from hence, because then he that had most of this would have most of God's image; and consequently Nimrod had more of it than Noah, Saul than Samuel, the persecutors than the martyrs, and Caesar than Christ Himself, which, to assert, is a, blasphemous paradox. And if the image of God is only grandeur, power, and sovereignty, certainly we have been hitherto much mistaken in our duty, and hereafter are by all means to beware of making ourselves unlike God by too much self-denial and humility. I am not ignorant that some may distinguish between a lawful authority and actual power, and affirm that God's image consists only in the former, which wicked princes, such, as Saul and Nimrod, have not, tho they possess the latter. But to this I answer,

1. That the Scripture neither makes nor owns such a distinction, nor anywhere asserts that when princes begin to be wicked they cease of right to be governors. Add to this, that when God renewed this charter of man's sovereignty over the creatures to Noah and his family we find no exception at all, but that Shem stood as fully invested with this right as any of his brethren.

2. But, secondly, this savors of something ranker than Socinianism, even the tenants of the fifth monarchy, and of sovereignty founded only upon saintship, and therefore fitter to be answered by the judge than the divine, and to receive its confutation at the bar of justice than from the pulpit.

Having now made our way through this false opinion, we are in the next place to lay down positively what this image of God in man is. It is, in short, that universal rectitude of all the faculties of the soul, by which they stand apt and disposed to their respective offices and operations, which will be more fully set forth by taking a distinct survey of it in the several faculties belonging to the soul.

1. In the understanding. 2. In the will. 3. In the passions or affections.

I. And, first, for its noblest faculty, the understanding: it was then sublime, clear, and aspiring—and, as it were, the soul's upper region, lofty and serene, free from vapors and disturbances of the inferior affections. It was the leading, controlling faculty; all the passions wore the colors of reason; it was not consul, but dictator. Discourse was then almost as quick as intuition; it was nimble in proposing, firm in concluding; it could sooner determine than now it can dispute. Like the sun, it had both light and agility; it knew no rest but in motion, no quiet but in activity. It did not so properly apprehend, as irradiate the object; not so much find, as make things intelligible. It did not arbitrate upon the several reports of sense, and all the varieties of imagination, like a drowsy judge, not only hearing, but also directing their verdict. In sum, it was vegete, quick, and lively, open as the day, untainted as the morning, full of the innocence and sprightliness of youth, it gave the soul a bright and a full view into all things, and was not only a window, but itself the prospect. Briefly, there is as much difference between the clear representations of the understanding then and the obscure discoveries that it makes now as there is between the prospect of a casement and of a keyhole.

Now, as there are two great functions of the soul, contemplation and practise, according to that general division of objects, some of which only entertain our speculation, others also employ our actions, so the understanding, with relation to these, not because of any distinction in the faculty itself, is accordingly divided into speculative and practical; in both of which the image of God was then apparent.

1. For the understanding speculative. There are some general maxims and notions in the mind of man which are the rules of discourse and the basis of all philosophy: as, that the same thing

can not at the same time be and not be; that the whole is bigger than a part; that two dimensions, severally equal to a third, must also be equal to one another. Aristotle, indeed, affirms the mind to be at first a mere *tabula rasa*, and that these notions are not ingenit, and imprinted by the finger of nature, but by the later and more languid impressions of sense, being only the reports of observation, and the result of so many repeated experiments.

(1.) That these notions are universal, and what is universal must needs proceed from some universal, constant principle, the same in all particulars, which here can be nothing else but human nature.

(2.) These can not be infused by observation, because they are the rules by which men take their first apprehensions and observations of things, and therefore, in order of nature, must needs precede them; as the being of the rule must be before its application to the thing directed by it. From whence it follows that these were notions not descending from us, but born with us, not our offspring, but our brethren; and, as I may so say, such as we were taught without the help of a teacher.

Now it was Adam's happiness in the state of innocence to have these clear and unsullied. He came into the world a philosopher, which sufficiently appeared by his writing the nature of things upon their names; he could view essences in themselves, and read forms without the comment of their respective properties; he could see consequents yet dormant in their principles, and effects yet unborn and in the womb of their causes; his understanding could almost pierce into future contingents; his conjectures improving even to prophecy, or the certainties of prediction; till his fall, it was ignorant of nothing but sin, or at least it rested in the notion, without the smart of the experiment. Could any difficulty have been proposed, the resolution would have been as early as the proposal; it could not have had time to settle into doubt. Like a better Archimedes, the issue of all his inquiries was a *eureka*, a *eureka*, the offspring of his brain without the sweat of his brow. Study was not then a duty, night-watchings were needless, the light of reason wanted not the assistance of a candle. This is the doom of fallen man, to labor in the fire, to seek truth *in profundo*, to exhaust his time and impair his health, and perhaps to spin out his days and himself into one pitiful, controverted conclusion. There was then no poring, no struggling with memory, no straining for invention; his faculties were quick and expedite, they answered without knocking, they were ready upon the first summons.

2. The image of God was no less resplendent in that which we call man's practical understanding; namely, that storehouse of the soul in which are treasured up the rules of action, and the seeds of morality; where, we must observe, that many who deny all connate notions in the speculative intellect, do yet admit them in this. Now of this sort are these maxims, "That God is to be worshiped, that parents are to be honored, that a man's word is to be kept," and the like; which, being of universal influence, as to the regulation of the behavior and converse of mankind, are the ground of all virtue and civility, and the foundation of religion.

It was the privilege of Adam innocent, to have these notions also firm and untainted, to carry his monitor in his bosom, his law in his heart, and to have such a conscience as might be its own casuist; and certainly those actions must needs be regular where there is an identity between the rule and the faculty. His own mind taught him a due dependence upon God, and chalked out to him the just proportions and measures of behavior to his fellow creatures. He had no catechism but the creation, needed no study but reflection, read no book but the volume of the world, and that too, not for the rules to work by, but for the objects to work upon. Reason was his tutor, and first principles his *magna moralia*. The decalogue of Moses was but a transcript, not an original. All the laws of nations, and wise decrees of states, the statutes of Solon, and the twelve tables, were but a paraphrase upon this standing rectitude of nature, this fruitful principle of justice, that was ready to run out and enlarge itself into suitable demonstrations upon all emergent objects and occasions.

And this much for the image of God, as it shone in man's understanding.

II. Let us in the next place take a view of it as it was stamped upon the will. It is much disputed by divines concerning the power of man's will to good and evil in the state of innocence: and upon very nice and dangerous precipices stand their determinations on either side. Some hold that God invested him with a power to stand so that in the strength of that power received, he might, without the auxiliaries of any further influence, have determined his will to a full choice of good. Others hold that notwithstanding this power, yet it was impossible for him to exert it in any good action without a superadded assistance of grace actually determining that power to the certain production of such an act; so that whereas some distinguish between sufficient and effectual grace, they order the matter so as to acknowledge some sufficient but what is indeed effected, and actually productive of good action. I shall not presume to interpose dogmatically in a controversy which I look never to see decided. But concerning the latter of these opinions, I shall only give these two remarks:

1. That it seems contrary to the common and natural conceptions of all mankind, who acknowledge themselves able and sufficient to do many things which actually they never do.

2. That to assert that God looked upon Adam's fall as a sin, and punished it as such when, without any antecedent sin of his, he withdrew that actual grace from him upon the withdrawing of which it was impossible for him not to fall, seems a thing that highly reproaches the essential equity and goodness of the divine nature.

Wherefore, doubtless the will of man in the state of innocence had an entire freedom, a perfect equipendency and indifference to either part of the contradiction, to stand, or not to stand; to accept, or not to accept the temptation. I will grant the will of man now to be as much a slave as any one who will have it, and be only free to sin; that is, instead of a liberty, to have only a licentiousness; yet certainly this is not nature, but chance. We were not born crooked; we learned these windings and turnings of the serpent: and therefore it can not but be a blasphemous piece of ingratitude to ascribe them to God, and to make the plague of our nature the condition of our creation.

The will was then ductile and pliant to all the motions of right reason; it met the dictates of a clarified understanding half way. And the active informations of the intellect, filling the passive reception of the will, like form closing with matter, grew actuate into a third and distinct perfection of practise; the understanding and will never disagreed; for the proposals of the one never thwarted the inclinations of the other. Yet neither did the will servilely attend upon the understanding, but as a favorite does upon his prince, where the service is privilege and preferment; or as Solomon's servants waited upon him: it admired its wisdom, and heard its prudent dictates and counsels—both the direction and the reward of its obedience. It is indeed the nature of this faculty to follow a superior guide—to be drawn by the intellect; but then it was drawn as a triumphant chariot, which at the same time both follows and triumphs: while it obeyed this, it commanded the other faculties. It was subordinate, not enslaved to the understanding: not as a servant to a master, but as a queen to her king, who both acknowledges a subjection and yet retains a majesty.

III. Pass we now downward from man's intellect and will to the passions, which have their residence and situation chiefly in the sensitive appetite. For we must know that inasmuch as man is a compound, and mixture of flesh as well as spirit, the soul, during its abode in the body, does all things by the mediation of these passions and inferior affections. And here the opinion of the Stoics was famous and singular, who looked upon all these as sinful defects and irregularities, as so many deviations from right reason, making passion to be only another word for perturbation. Sorrow in their esteem was a sin scarce to be expiated by another; to pity, was a fault; to rejoice, an extravagance; and the apostle's advice, "to be angry and sin not," was a contradiction in their philosophy. But in this they were constantly outvoted by other sects of philosophers, neither for fame nor number less than themselves: so that all arguments brought against them from divinity would come in by way of overplus to their confutation. To us let this be sufficient, that our Savior Christ, who took upon Him all our natural infirmities, but none of our sinful, has been seen to weep, to be sorrowful, to pity, and to be angry: which shows that there might be gall in a dove, passion without sin, fire without smoke, and motion without disturbance. For it is not bare agitation, but the sediment at the bottom, that troubles and defiles the water; and when we see it windy and dusty, the wind does not (as we used to say) make, but only raise a dust.

Now, tho the schools reduce all the passions to these two heads, the concupiscible and the irascible appetite, yet I shall not tie myself to an exact prosecution of them under this division; but at this time, leaving both their terms and their method to themselves, consider only the principal and noted passions, from whence we may take an estimate of the rest.

And first for the grand leading affection of all, which is love. This is the great instrument and engine of nature, the bond and cement of society, the spring and spirit of the universe. Love is such an affection as can not so properly be said to be in the soul as the soul to be in that. It is the whole man wrapt up into one desire; all the powers, vigor, and faculties of the soul abridged into one inclination. And it is of that active, restless nature that it must of necessity exert itself; and, like the fire to which it is so often compared, it is not a free agent, to choose whether it will heat or no, but it streams forth by natural results and unavoidable emanations. So that it will fasten upon any inferior, unsuitable object, rather than none at all. The soul may sooner leave off to subsist than to love; and, like the vine, it withers and dies if it has nothing to embrace. Now this affection, in the state of innocence, was happily pitched upon its right object; it flamed up in direct fervors of devotion to God, and in collateral emissions of charity to its neighbor. It was not then only another and more

171

cleanly name for lust. It had none of those impure heats that both represent and deserve hell. It was a vestal and a virgin fire, and differed as much from that which usually passes by this name nowadays as the vital heat from the burning of a fever.

Then for the contrary passion of hatred. This we know is the passion of defiance, and there is a kind of aversation and hostility included in its very essence and being. But then (if there could have been hatred in the world when there was scarce anything odious) it would have acted within the compass of its proper object; like aloes, bitter indeed, but wholesome. There would have been no rancor, no hatred of our brother: an innocent nature could hate nothing that was innocent. In a word, so great is the commutation that the soul then hated only that which now only it loves, that is, sin.

And if we may bring anger under this head, as being, according to some, a transient hatred, or at least very like it, this also, as unruly as now it is, yet then it vented itself by the measures of reason. There was no such thing as the transports of malice or the violences of revenge, no rendering evil for evil, when evil was truly a nonentity and nowhere to be found. Anger, then, was like the sword of justice, keen, but innocent and righteous: it did not act like fury, then call itself zeal. It always espoused God's honor, and never kindled upon anything but in order to a sacrifice. It sparkled like the coal upon the altar with the fervors of piety, the heats of devotion, the sallies and vibrations of a harmless activity.

In the next place, for the lightsome passion of joy. It was not that which now often usurps this name; that trivial, vanishing, superficial thing, that only gilds the apprehension and plays upon the surface of the soul. It was not the mere crackling of thorns or sudden blaze of the spirits, the exultation of a tickled fancy or a pleased appetite. Joy was then a masculine and a severe thing; the recreation of the judgment, the jubilee of reason. It was the result of a real good, suitably applied. It commenced upon the solidity of truth and the substance of fruition. It did not run out in voice or indecent eruptions, but filled the soul, as God does the universe, silently and without noise. It was refreshing, but composed, like the pleasantness of youth tempered with the gravity of age; or the mirth of a festival managed with the silence of contemplation.

And, on the other side, for sorrow: Had any loss or disaster made but room for grief, it would have moved according to the severe allowances of prudence, and the proportions of the provocation. It would not have sallied out into complaint of loudness, nor spread itself upon the face, and writ sad stories upon the forehead. No wringing of hands, knocking the breast, or wishing oneself unborn; all which are but the ceremonies of sorrow, the pomp and ostentation of an effeminate grief, which speak not so much the greatness of the misery as the smallness of the mind! Tears may spoil the eyes, but not wash away the affliction. Sighs may exhaust the man, but not eject the burden. Sorrow, then, would have been as silent as thought, as severe as philosophy. It would have been rested in inward senses, tacit dislikes; and the whole scene of it been transacted in sad and silent reflections....

And, lastly, for the affection of fear: It was then the instrument of caution, not of anxiety; a guard, and not a torment to the breast that had it. It is now indeed an unhappiness, the disease of the soul: it flies from a shadow, and makes more dangers than it avoids; it weakens the judgment and betrays the succors of reason: so hard is it to tremble and not to err, and to hit the mark with a shaking hand. Then it fixt upon Him who is only to be feared, God; and yet with a filial fear, which at the same time both fears and loves. It was awe without amazement, dread without distraction. There was then a beauty even in this very paleness. It was the color of devotion, giving a luster to reverence and a gloss to humility.

Thus did the passions then act without any of their present jars, combats, or repugnances; all moving with the beauty of uniformity and the stillness of composure; like a well-governed army, not for fighting, but for rank and order. I confess the

Scripture does not expressly attribute these several endowments to Adam in his first estate. But all that I have said, and much more, may be drawn out of that short aphorism, "God made man upright." And since the opposite weaknesses infest the nature of man fallen, if we will be true to the rules of contraries we must conclude that these perfections were the lot of man innocent....

Having thus surveyed the image of God in the soul of man, we are not to omit now those characters of majesty that God imprinted upon the body. He drew some traces of His image upon this also, as much as a spiritual substance could be pictured upon a corporeal. As for the sect of the Anthropomorphites, who from hence ascribe to God the figure of a man, eyes, hands, feet, and the like, they are too ridiculous to deserve a confutation. They would seem to draw this impiety from the letter of the Scripture sometimes speaking of God in this manner. Absurdity! as if the mercy of Scripture expressions ought to warrant the blasphemy of our opinions; and not rather to show us that God condescends to us only to draw us to Himself; and clothes Himself in our likeness only to win us to His own. The practise of the papists is much of the same nature, in their absurd and impious picturing of God Almighty; but the wonder in them is the less since the image of a deity may be a proper object for that which is but the image of a religion. But to the purpose: Adam was then no less glorious in his externals; he had a beautiful body, as well as an immortal soul. The whole compound was like a well-built temple, stately without, and sacred within. The elements were at perfect union and agreement in His body; and their contrary qualities served not for the dissolution of the compound, but the variety of the composure. Galen, who had no more divinity than what his physic taught him, barely upon the consideration of this so exact frame of the body, challenges any one, upon a hundred years' study, to find out how any the least fiber, or most minute particle, might be more commodiously placed, either for the advantage of use or comeliness. His stature erect, and tending upward to his center; his countenance majestic and comely, with the luster of a native beauty that scorned the poor assistance of art or the attempts of imitation; His body of so much quickness and agility that it did not only contain but also represent the soul; for we might well suppose that where God did deposit so rich a jewel He would suitably adorn the case. It was a fit workhouse for sprightly, vivid faculties to exercise and exert themselves in; a fit tabernacle for an immortal soul, not only to dwell in, but to contemplate upon; where it might see the world without travel, it being a lesser scheme of the creation, nature contracted a little cosmography or map of the universe. Neither was the body then subject to distempers, to die by piecemeal, and languish under coughs, catarrhs, or consumptions. Adam knew no disease so long as temperance from the forbidden fruit secured him. Nature was his physician, and innocence and abstinence would have kept him healthful to immortality.

The two great perfections that both adorn and exercise man's understanding, are philosophy and religion: for the first of these, take it even among the professors of it where it most flourished, and we shall find the very first notions of common-sense debauched by them. For there have been such as have asserted, "that there is no such thing in the world as motion: that contradictions may be true." There has not been wanting one that has denied snow to be white. Such a stupidity or wantonness had seized upon the most raised wits that it might be doubted whether the philosophers or the owls of Athens were the quicker sighted. But then for religion; what prodigious, monstrous, misshapen births has the reason of fallen man produced! It is now almost six thousand years that far the greater part of the world has had no other religion but idolatry: and idolatry certainly is the first-born of folly, the great and leading paradox, nay, the very abridgment and sum total of all absurdities. For is it not strange that a rational man should worship an ox, nay, the image of an ox? That he should fawn upon his dog? Bow himself before a cat? Adore leeks and garlic, and shed penitential tears at the smell of a deified onion? Yet so did the Egyptians, once the famed masters of all arts and learning. And to go a little further, we have yet a stronger instance in Isaiah, "A man hews him down a tree in the wood, and a part of it he burns, with the residue thereof he maketh a god." With one part he furnishes his chimney, with the other his chapel. A strange thing that the fire must first consume this part and then burn incense to that. As if there was more divinity in one end of the stick than in the other; or, as if he could be graved and painted omnipotent, or the nails and the hammer could give it an apotheosis! Briefly, so great is the change, so deplorable the degradation of our nature, that whereas we bore the image of God, we now retain only the image of man.

In the last place, we learn hence the excellency of Christian religion, in that it is the great and only means that God has sanctified and designed to repair the breaches of humanity, to set fallen man upon his legs again, to clarify his reason, to rectify his will, and to compose and regulate his affections. The whole business of our redemption is, in short, only to rub over the defaced copy of the creation, to reprint God's image upon the soul, and, as it were, to set forth nature in a second and fairer edition; the recovery of which lost image, as it is God's pleasure to command, and our duty to endeavor, so it is in His power only to effect; to whom be rendered and ascribed, as is most due, all praise, might, majesty, and dominion, both now and forever more. Amen.

END OF VOL. II.